DESIGN IN THE BUILT ENVIRONMENT

DESIGN
IN THE BUILT ENVIRONMENT

R. FRASER REEKIE
Chartered Town Planner
Chartered Architect
Urban Designer

Edward Arnold

© R. FRASER REEKIE 1972

First published 1972
by Edward Arnold (Publishers) Ltd.
25 Hill Street
London WIX 8LL

ISBN: 0 7131 3268 X Boards
ISBN: 0 7131 3275 2 Paper

Printed in Great Britain by
Fletcher & Son Ltd, Norwich

Author's Preface

This book has been written primarily as an introduction and a guide to the study and understanding of design in the built environment, with particular emphasis on visual effects.

There are many existing books on town and country planning, sometimes referred to as urban and regional planning, and on architecture; and more are published every month. But, so far as I am aware, there is no book that sets out simply and in a straightforward manner, as this book is intended to do, the fundamentals of its subject. Such basic knowledge is essential, not only to students of planning and architecture, who will pursue the subject further in greater depth and detail, but also to students of surveying, building and engineering, and to others, who in any way are directly concerned with the creation of man's physical surroundings. And not only to those who are professionally or technically concerned, but to everyone — legislators, developers and the general public — who should intelligently participate in the urgent task of abolishing ugliness, dreariness, squalor, and all offensiveness from towns, villages and countryside, and in restoring and producing visual pleasure in the environment, so that life can be lived therein more healthily and happily.

One of the points made in this book is that environmental design, now and in the future, is and will be a matter of expert teamwork supported by public appreciation. Some members of a team may have a greater degree of responsibility in certain respects than others, but everyone should be agreed on the aims and the broad means of achieving them. Each individual can rightly have his or her idea of what is beautiful in landscape, townscape and buildings, but personal subjective evaluations, although eminently worth expounding and discussing, are nevertheless irrelevant in the context of design that is for the benefit of all. The day may never come, and perhaps just as well, when visual aspects of design will be quantified and run through an electronic computer to find out if they are satisfactory, but there is no reason why valid objective assessments should not be made by the human brain, provided there are agreed standards of good design. It is a theme of this book that such general and universally applicable standards can be established and that, in accordance with those principles, judgements can be exercised and decisions made that will ensure combined environmental efficiency and amenity.

The views expressed in detail in the text are sincerely held by the author, but as he lays no claim to infallibility, where the word 'should' or 'must' occurs, it can be understood to be followed by: 'in the opinion of the author'. To have printed this phrase every time would have been tedious.

Because there is at present a good deal of verbal inconsistency in English, especially as regards inter-disciplinary jargon – the word 'environment', for example, has various meanings – I have tried to keep the text clear from ambiguity by giving one meaning to each word throughout, except when the sense prevents misunderstanding, and by avoiding the over-use of multi-syllabic or what my West Indian friends call 'five-dollar' words! A glossary of words and terms is also provided as an appendix.

A number of blank pages are included at the end for notes, sketches and cuttings so that pertinent material can be added by the student. While the fundamental principles will be slow to change, or change at all, designs are continually and rapidly changing because of new social needs, fluctuating economic conditions and technological advances in many fields. Students who are interested in furthering their study of the subject are advised to use folders or scrapbooks, one for each chapter heading and principal subsections, for the collection of additional material. Reference books are not listed in this work; it is better if lists are obtained from local and national libraries, including those of professional and technical institutions and associations. And remember, good and bad actual examples to be looked at, examined, considered and compared, are all around you.

In conclusion, I would like to thank all those, known and unknown, who have assisted me, many unwittingly, with the preparation of this book. Friends, colleagues and students, thank you very much.

R. FRASER REEKIE

Contents

Illustrations, Acknowledgements and Credits

Drawings

All drawings, with the exception of the plan on p. 71, which was made by Michael Preston, were prepared by the author.

Drawings of traffic signs on p. 17 are reproduced by permission of Controller, H.M. Stationery Office.

Diagram of Residential Area on p. 68 after illustration in "The Prospect for Housing" prepared by Colin Buchanan and Partners for the Nationwide Building Society.

Photographs

p. 21	Tapiola, Finland	Fraser Reekie ⎫ Colour
	Wiltshire Downs	Fraser Reekie ⎭
p. 24	Coleg Harlech, Hall of Residence, Harlech (Colwyn, Foulkes & Partners, Architects)	Fraser Reekie
p. 28	Bank Building, Port of Spain	Fraser Reekie
	Nurses Hostel, Pointe a Pierre	Fraser Reekie
p. 29	Office Building, London	Courtesy: British Steel Corporation
	Shop, Oxford Street, London	Courtesy: Mothercare Limited
p. 34	Office Building and Shopping Centre, Coventry	Fraser Reekie
	Hotel, Bristol	Fraser Reekie
	Office Buildings, Toronto	Fraser Reekie
p. 35	Hotel, Trinidad	Courtesy: Industrial Development Corpn., Trinidad
p. 39	Library, Stevenage	Fraser Reekie
	Multi-storey Building, Coventry	Fraser Reekie
	Coleg Harlech, Hall of Residence, Harlech	Fraser Reekie
p. 40	La Grande Motte, France	Courtesy: French Tourist Office
	Geodesic Dome, Montreal	Alan Reekie

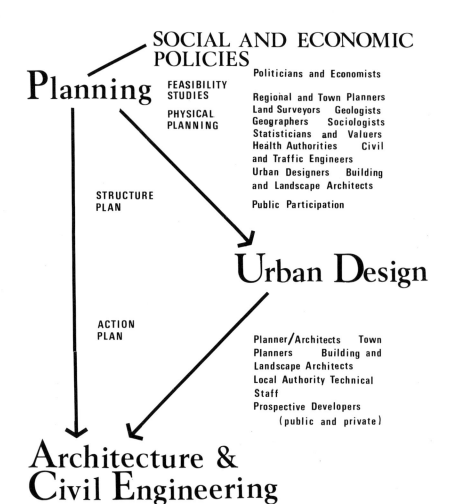

Planning

SOCIAL AND ECONOMIC POLICIES

FEASIBILITY STUDIES

PHYSICAL PLANNING

STRUCTURE PLAN

ACTION PLAN

Politicians and Economists

Regional and Town Planners
Land Surveyors   Geologists
Geographers   Sociologists
Statisticians and Valuers
Health Authorities   Civil
and Traffic Engineers
Urban Designers   Building
and Landscape Architects

Public Participation

Urban Design

Planner/Architects   Town
Planners   Building and
Landscape Architects
Local Authority Technical
Staff
Prospective Developers
     (public and private)

Architecture & Civil Engineering

SPECIFIC PROJECT

Building Designers and/or
Professional Engineers
Developers   and   Clients
Structural and Mechanical
Engineers   Land and
Quantity Surveyors
Landscape Architects
Constructional Specialists
                        etc

THE BUILT ENVIRONMENT
STAGES OF DESIGN

1
Introduction

Built environment

By 'built environment' is meant that part of the physical surroundings which are man-made or man-organised, such as buildings and other major structures, roads, bridges, and the like, down to lesser objects such as traffic control signals and telephone boxes. They are the things used and seen in everyday life. In large concentrations, including many dwellings, they constitute towns; in smaller collections they form villages and hamlets; they occur, more or less dispersed, throughout the countryside in all but the most remote and undeveloped areas.

Design

'Design' is a word of many meanings, some of which are imprecise and misleading. Here, with particular reference to planning and buildings, i.e. environmental design and urban design, a meaning is adopted that can apply to anything that is used and can be seen: the conscious or intentional putting together or the shaping of materials to meet certain needs.

This definition implies two considerations: firstly, the establishing and clarifying of the requirements or needs. This may be, for example, in respect of a new door-handle or of a vastly more complicated new town. And secondly, decisions as to the best means of physical realisation within prevailing circumstances.

The first consideration has two aspects:.there is the aspect of practical use, e.g. the door-handle is required conveniently to operate the mechanism that holds the door in the closed position, and there is the visual aspect. The visual aspect, that is the appearance of the door-handle or of the town, or whatever is the object, is equally important. It is not sufficient that the object functions satisfactorily; its appearance must be visually satisfactory. Indeed, appearance may be an essential part of purpose or use, either in

1

evoking some emotional response in the viewer, or in conveying or reinforcing practical function, as with directional signs or distinguishing colours.

Aesthetics

A distinction has to be made between the term 'visually satisfactory' and the word 'aesthetic'. The latter should properly be used in regard to beauty – a special and intense visual quality. But beauty is subjective. What one person finds beautiful, another may find unattractive or positively ugly. Most people of any race, beliefs or education will agree on the beauty of a sunset, a flower or other natural phenomena, but individuals are likely to disagree, perhaps strongly, on the degree of beauty of a particular building, painting or piece of sculpture. This is because personal subjective reactions are conditioned by upbringing, past experiences and associations, the influences of others and even, in some cases, a sublime belief in divinely-inspired ability to define beauty !

But visual satisfaction results from the objective appreciation of the appearance of towns, buildings and objects which are well-designed in accordance with generally accepted basic principles. Although immediate reactions cannot be ignored – first impressions do matter, but they are transitory and necessarily superficial – intelligent judgement must go deeper. An ill-placed, badly built, inconvenient and insanitary shack seen from afar when illuminated by golden sunlight might fortuitously look beautiful, but it would be nonsense to say that it is therefore a well-designed building. Conversely, the first sight of a really well-designed building seen on a grey, cold and wet day may be depressing and unbeautiful, but it would be unfair to judge the building by subjective reaction at that moment in time.

Principles of design

To make an objective assessment of a design, or to set about the process of designing, consideration has to be given to the three aspects mentioned in the foregoing and which may be summarised as :

1. Function: the satisfying of requirements of use or purpose;
2. Structure: the physical implementation of function by the best available material(s), construction, manufacture and skills as conditions permit;
3. Appearance: the obtaining of satisfactory visual effects (sometimes referred to as 'aesthetic values').

Other words can be used to describe these three aspects but on analysis, whatever words are used, it will be found that almost every writer on building design, which may be extended to cover the built environment, is dealing with the same three fundamentals.

These three constituent parts of design are closely interrelated and each to a greater or less extent, according to the nature of the subject, influences the others. An urban composition or a building or a detail that is truly well-designed is one in the creation of which all three aspects have been fully considered and integrated.

Integration may well be the key-word in good design. Not only does it mean the correct combining of parts into a whole, but it implies, by association with integrity, soundness and honesty.

2
The Design Process

Designs of towns, urban developments and of buildings and related objects are produced nowadays by the corporate efforts of trained and qualified professionals: town-planners, urban designers, building architects and civil engineers, assisted by various consultants and specialists, all working together in systematic and logical ways. Such groups or consortia are referred to as *design teams*. For the physical implementation of designs – and no design is complete until it is a reality – other groups which, in addition to containing certain members of the design teams also contain contractors, manufacturers and technical experts, are known as *construction* or *production teams*.

Design teams

It is convenient to regard design of the built environment as consisting of three parts: (1) planning; (2) urban design; (3) building design. Planning, in this division, is the general disposition of land areas for various uses, the general location of buildings and open spaces, and provisions for services and surface communications, expressed more or less in a two-dimensional manner.

Urban design is the more specific laying out of roads and buildings and other urban elements with regard both to efficiency and visual effect; for example, the general arrangement of building masses and the preservation and enhancement of amenities considered three-dimensionally.

Building design is the detail design, including constructional materials and methods, of individual and groups of buildings, and of structures such as civil engineering works, within the context of the overall planning scheme and urban design. These three parts of environmental design are not separate and distinct. Planning, although many other matters have to be taken into account, cannot be properly carried out without consideration of the subsequent stages of urban design and building design; urban design, which is conditioned by planning, is a preliminary to building design. Indeed, in practice the person controlling planning may act also as the leader of the urban design team, and the composition of the urban design team may be substantially the same as that of the building design team, although not necessarily so. However, no responsible architect would today design a building without relating it to its environment. Design teams must each have a leader or director to inspire, organise and co-ordinate all activities, and to make final decisions. Planning teams usually have qualified town-planners at the head; urban design teams have planner/architects, i.e. a planner with an architectural qualification, or vice versa!; and building design teams have architects or professional engineers. Such men often attain eminence in their respective fields, and unquestionably, personal ability and special qualities are major factors in the successful achievements with which they are associated. Nevertheless, all but the most conceited would freely admit their debt to team-work and the co-operation of others. Present-day complexities of required information and background knowledge, and of the problems and sub-problems to be solved in connection with almost all major design projects, are too far beyond the experiences and capabilities of any individual designer to cope with alone.

Planning teams. Town-planners or urban and regional planners are the principal members of the planning team. Among the supporting consultants and specialists to whom reference is made for information, advice and criticism are: land surveyors, urban designers, building and landscape architects, civil and traffic engineers, lawyers, economists, sociologists, geographers, statisticians and mathematicians, and central and local government officials. On a different level, reference may also be made to the general public. The respective contributions will vary according to circumstances, and the nature and extent of the proposed design, and although in some cases the contributions may be minor, they are always important. The success of a design and of its ultimate realisation must depend on it satisfying all subjects and matters in any way involved, so far as it is practicable to do so.

Urban design teams. Architect/planners or urban designers are the leaders. They work with town-planners, land surveyors, estate managers, civil engineers, building and landscape architects, the technical staff of local authorities, and with prospective developers.

Building design teams. Generally, architects are the principals, either official or privately commissioned. They operate within the requirements of planning schemes and building regulations, and within urban guide-lines, either self-determined or determined by others, and in co-operation with various specialists, e.g. land surveyors, structural and mechanical engineers, electrical, water supply and drainage and heating and ventilating engineers,

quantity surveyors, interior designers, acoustic experts, landscape architects and, possibly, building contractors, manufacturers and suppliers of
materials and fittings. For civil engineering designs, specialist engineers
appropriate to the project, e.g. highways, bridges, harbours or tunnels,
similarly lead and co-operate with other professionals and technical
experts.

Design methods

In the past, the process of designing was vaguely believed to be largely
a subconscious activity by 'gifted' individuals – a matter of intuition –
which has been described, perhaps accurately, as non-thinking! This belief, which makes good journalistic copy and is much used for publicity
purposes, may have been tenable to some extent when buildings and layouts were relatively simple or were dealt with in isolation, and when
appearance was judged as something apart from function and construction.
But, in more recent times, it has become clear that the problems of the
present and the future cannot be grasped much less solved by unreliable
and capricious intuition. This must be so considering the increasing com-
plexity of town-planning and building design requirements, coupled with
modern technology, and the growing realisation that all parts of the built
environment must be interrelated, and that for true visual satisfaction
appearance must be integrated with functional arrangement and its physical
implementation. Consequently, attention is now paid to the formulation of
design methods (design methodology or system design), which are disciplined ways of designing by teams or groups, as previously described, as
opposed to the 'doodling' or murky mystique approach. Parallel with this
search for the most effective design techniques is research into the
psychology of thought and decision-making.

On the one hand, therefore, there is the examination of the practical
organisation of information, analyses and selections, and finally therefrom
the emergence of a satisfactory design; and on the other, an enquiry into
mental processes of individuals and teams during such a design process, the
object being to arrive at a framework of procedure within which imaginative
and creative ideas can be freely generated and most effectively controlled
and utilised to the desired end in reasonable time.

Before suggesting a plan of work applicable to the majority of projects
it is of interest to outline former ways of design:

1. Primitive designers no doubt used materials which were readily available, such as clay, stones, wood, even snow, and found ways of
   making things and constructing shelters by trial and error or by the
   pragmatic approach.

2. From the pragmatic approach would develop a degree of standardisation. It would be found, as it still is, that certain arrangements,
   materials and techniques were more satisfactory than others for
   ordinary uses in similar conditions, and designs embodying them
   would become 'fixed'. In time, they would be accepted as 'right' or
   'correct' designs and would become ossified in tradition. Designs
   based thereon are known as *iconic* – an image of a conventional type.
3. However, designs cannot remain static for ever (although they can
   persist for very long periods) and, with the development of skills and
   desire for better living conditions, new materials and new methods
   would supersede the older ones but form and detail would be trans-
   lated from the earlier types. As examples, in Ancient Egypt, the stone
   buildings show features derived from mud and reed walls and huts;
   in Ancient Greece, the later marble temples are clearly developments
   from timber prototypes. This kind of design is given the word
   analogous – similar to.
4. When drawings began to be used as a means of formulating designs
   and testing ideas before actual setting out or commencing construction, there would be a tendency for draughtsmanship to influence
   design, e.g. layouts and buildings became geometrical and symmetrical. A similar effect may be exerted on design in the future by the
   use of digital computers which reduce the process to yes/no or on/off
   decisions.

   Development of skill in drawing would later give rise, along with
   other causes, to the notion that there might be a mathematical or
   geometrical basis of design. Laws of proportion were sought from
   Greek times onwards, and still exert a kind of fascination: this aspect
   design is dealt with in a later chapter. Attempts to design in accordance
   with such laws or rules, supposedly of a mystic nature, are called
   canonic.
5. Canonic design is concerned mainly with external appearance. It pre-
   determines patterns of layouts, shapes of open spaces and the façades
   of buildings. In contrast, so-called *rational design* rightly paid
   attention to the analysis of function as a basis for decisions on
   planning, at a time when the arrangement of parts and construction
   were still relatively simple, but had little effect on outward appearance
   which remained, at the period in question, a dressing up in past styles.
   To some, Ancient Greek and Roman trappings were termed classical
   as these civilisations were regarded as the fount of pure design; to
   others, Gothic or Medieval garb – regarded as 'Christian' art – and
   much miscellaneous historical copyism was preferred.

   In the last hundred years, however, with industrialisation and the
   rapid growth of towns, and because of the great technological

advances referred to in Chapter 11, urban and building design has burst out of the restricting methods of the past. While there is considerable merit in some of the town plans and individual buildings of previous times and valuable visual lessons to be learned from them, the design procedure of today must be comprehensive in scope and related to the whole environment.

Design procedure

There are many varieties of design procedure, but generally they are rationalisations, in one form or another, of an orderly step by step progression. The following is a broad outline of a basic system, which can be used in connection with design in the built environment. It is in four stages :

1. *Brief* – The first step in design procedure is always the clarification and thorough understanding of the design problem by the preparation of a brief or statement defining in detail the requirements of function, purpose and use – including the desired visual effect. It includes the range of materials, methods of construction or manufacture – if predetermined – the limitations of cost or other constraints and so on. This may be a simple matter, as in the case of a street sign, or it may be a considerable task, as in the case of a new town. Some information may be readily available from experience or may be recorded from earlier or similar designs ; some may be obtained from reliable sources such as libraries or data banks ; some may be contributed by specialist members of the design team or by outside consultants. It may sometimes be necessary for new research and investigations to be carried out. Everything that has or might reasonably have bearing on the problem should be collected.

   Also at this stage, a time-table should be drawn up and dates established, realistically but not generously for the virtual completion of further stages and the final completion of the design. A time-table is a great stimulus to mental activity !

2. *Analysis* – The second main stage, after establishing the brief and gathering relevant information, is the initial analysis of the problem into parts, that is into sub-problems, if the subject is big enough and is capable of division, and into the three basic aspects of (i) functional arrangement, (ii) materials and construction and (iii) visual effect. This is followed by the sorting of accumulated data and co-ordination of individual specialist contributions in relation to these parts.

   This is done so that solutions can be found that are full and complete in all respects. During the process, it may become apparent that additional information to that first obtained, is needed, or even that the brief requires modification. It may therefore be necessary to return

Brief
clarification of requirements, possibilities and constraints research and investigation

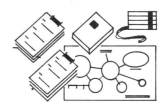

Analysis
sorting, evaluating and coordinating of information and specialists' contributions

Synthesis
progressive production of designs to viability testing and checking recycling

Implementation
presentation of final, complete design physical realisation...

Communication
verbal and graphic conveying of ideas, opinions and queries

DESIGN PROCEDURE

and reconsider the first stage before proceeding further. What is most important at the second stage is that all concerned are agreed upon the ultimate aim.

3. *Synthesis* – Solutions will begin to suggest themselves in the previous stage but now free rein is given to the production of actual designs in accordance with the essential preliminary steps already taken. This starts with freehand sketches and thence progresses, by means of more refined drawings and perhaps models made to full size or to appropriate scale as the subject warrants – working from general to detail requirements but with possibly some reciprocation – until all aspects have been met and the viability of the design seems assured.

The process may involve the evaluation, at some points, of alternative potential solutions, with a recycling back and forth to stages 1 and 2, and the checking against established criteria, and it will certainly require the making of decisions. It is here that the hard – but often pleasurable and exciting – work of designing is done. Knowledge, skill, imagination, and a steadfast adherence to basic principles are required for success. Ideas alone are not enough; they may come to anyone at any time. It is the ability to take ideas from their own or others minds and to assess them and, if helpful, to adopt, adapt, improve and combine them that distinguishes the true designers. Ideas are like diamonds: they are not brilliant until they have been cut, polished and set!

4 *Implementation* – The final stage is the preparation of the design in its perfected form, and its presentation by drawings, descriptions, models or any other appropriate means, so that it can be understood and appreciated, and in due course can be given physical realisation, i.e. it can be constructed or manufactured.

The initial letters of the words used to describe the foregoing four stages of design procedure are B A S I; if the letter C is added for 'Communication', the result is BASIC, a word that describes the whole operation: Basic Design Procedure.

Communication here refers to the means, verbal and graphic, whereby concepts and queries are conveyed and discussed between members of the design team. Incidentally, speaking and especially the act of drawing and making models, helps to generate ideas as well as express them.

3
Visual Design

The object of all planning and building design is the production of an environment for efficient and happy living. The starting-points for the designer are the natural and man-made world as it exists, and the needs and desires of people who live in it. The physical environment and its mental and emotional effects result in the main from perception through sight. Therefore the appearance of things, of buildings and other structures, of roads and open spaces of various kinds, is of great importance practically and psychologically. Visual design must be considered by all concerned from the beginning of the planning process through to the selection or detailing of minor items of street furniture. Appearance cannot be considered successfully as an after-thought, although remedial or cosmetic treatment to improve existing landscape and townscape may be possible in some cases, where insufficient thought was given to visual effects initially, or where neglect has brought about deterioration and decay. Knowledge of the phenomena of light and sight and of human responses to what is seen is essential to the understanding of basic principles of good visual design. The following is an introduction to what can be a continuing study to develop visual appreciation and perception, making possible the provision of increased practical efficiency and greater visual enjoyment and satisfaction in the designed environment.

Sight

Sight is the physical perception of light rays by the eye. The eye transforms the rays into sensations within the brain, which interprets them as:

'lines'   shapes   forms   colours   textures

which produce mental 'pictures' that are either new or recognisable, and these, in turn, cause certain reactions. The mechanics of vision – simplified –

are that rays of light, from an original or reflected source, pass through the pupil of the eye and are focused on to a concave surface at the rear of the eyeball, the retina, which has millions of sensitive spots (rods and cones). These spots are sensitive to different parts of light. If all the spots are activated, the sensation transmitted by the optic nerve to the brain is that of white light; if only the spots sensitive to the red part of light are activated, the sensation will be of red light. Colour-blindness, which to varying extent affects a number of people, is due to lack of sensitivity of the retina to certain light rays.

Light

Natural light or daylight – and moonlight – is sunlight; it originates from the sun. *Artificial light* may come from any one of a number of sources but is usually from some kind of electric lamp.

Diffused sunlight, i.e. through the atmosphere, is the accepted standard of *white* light, which is the whole of the visible waveband between 400 and 700 millimicrons. Light is a form of radiant energy and, although it is usual to speak of 'rays' of light because it is practical and convenient to do so, light actually travels in wave motion at about 186,000 miles per second in air. Light occupies only a narrow part of the range of radiation. Immediately beyond its waveband, below 400 millimicrons are the ultra-violet rays, and above 700 millimicrons are infra-red rays; neither of these are normally visible to the human eye.

White light contains all colours; literally, all the colours of the rainbow, which is caused by a refraction of sunlight due to moisture in the atmosphere. Similar effects can be seen in the spray of a waterfall or a fountain, or result when a beam of sunlight passes through a glass prism. When the light and the effect is strong, the colours: violet, indigo, blue, green, yellow, orange and red can be seen, although many people cannot see indigo. Often, only three or four colours are visible.

The partial splitting up of white light into some of the constituent colours is seen in the sky, especially early morning and late in the day, at sunrise and sunset, when atmospheric interference is at its maximum, and most of the shorter waves are absorbed or scattered and the longer waves, reds and yellows, predominate. When the sun is high in the sky, the reverse happens and on a clear day the sky appears blue.

Pure white light may be seen reflected from sea foam and cumulus clouds and from newly fallen snow, all in brilliant sunlight. Many other materials and surfaces are described as 'white' but by comparison with diffused sunlight are found to have a colour bias of one kind or another. As to be expected, white light can be reconstituted by mixing the colours of the rainbow but, as some of these colours are mixtures of others, only the

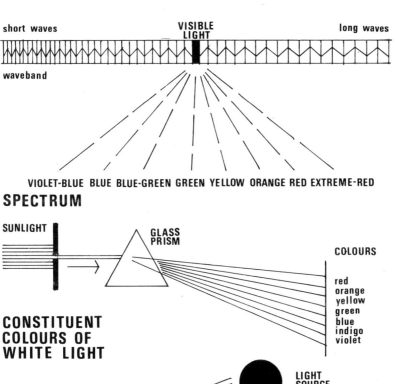

short waves   VISIBLE LIGHT   long waves

waveband

VIOLET-BLUE BLUE BLUE-GREEN GREEN YELLOW ORANGE RED EXTREME-RED

SPECTRUM

SUNLIGHT   GLASS PRISM

COLOURS

red
orange
yellow
green
blue
indigo
violet

CONSTITUENT COLOURS OF WHITE LIGHT

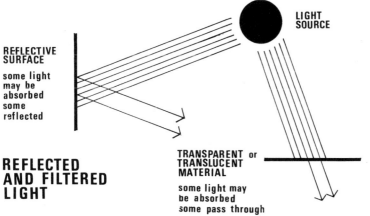

LIGHT SOURCE

REFLECTIVE SURFACE

some light
may be
absorbed
some
reflected

REFLECTED AND FILTERED LIGHT

TRANSPARENT or TRANSLUCENT MATERIAL

some light may
be absorbed
some pass through

LIGHT   DIAGRAMS

13

basic red, blue and green need be mixed; this can be done by focusing beams of such colours on to a point. But that is the direct mixing of coloured light. If pigments such as paints are mixed, the effect results from reflected light. To obtain an approximation of white light, the primary colours, which are red, blue and yellow can be applied in equal areas to the surface of a disc, which is then rapidly rotated. Mixing of lights increases brightness; mixing pigments has a darkening effect.

Environmental design is concerned almost wholly with reflected light from pigmented surfaces, either self-coloured or painted in some way.

From the primary colours, red, blue and yellow, the secondary colours, purple, orange and green can be obtained by mixing; i.e. red + blue = purple; red + yellow = orange; blue + yellow = green. By further mixing in different combinations and various proportions an enormous range of colours can be obtained. In nature and in artificial materials of all kinds such colours, some of great subtlety can be identified.

Pigmented surfaces, natural or artificial, absorb or subtract some of the light that falls upon them. If the light is white – not all light is white – then a yellow surface is one that absorbs the blue part of white light and reflects green and red, which together are perceived by the eye as yellow. A white surface would reflect all the light falling upon it. A black surface absorbs all light and reflects back nothing – such a surface is seldom found, although near-black surfaces are described as black.

Light can also be transformed by passing through filters, which absorb some wavelengths while permitting others to continue, e.g. stained and coloured glass and translucent plastic materials in windows.

Another kind of reflection results from surfaces which do not absorb part of the light but interfere with and change the wavelengths, e.g. iridescence – feathers, oil film on water and fluorescence.

Artificial light

In the design of the built environment, consideration should always be given to artificial lighting in regard to general illumination of roads and open spaces for convenience and safety, and for special purposes, such as the floodlighting of buildings, traffic and directional signs, advertising, etc. as referred to in later chapters. Account has also to be taken of the internal lighting of buildings when this can be seen from outside, and when it illuminates the immediate surroundings, whether intended or not. Most artificial light differs from daylight in quality, and it seldom contains the balance of colours found in standard white light, although the eye compensates for deficiences to some extent.

Examples of sources of artificial light are:

1. The *tungsten filament electric lamp*, e.g. the ordinary incandescent bulb which is still perhaps the most common type. The emitted light tends towards orange, so that surfaces that appear blue in daylight look weaker and greyish when seen by such light. However, psychologically, it is a comfortable light.
2. *Fluorescent tubes*; the colour characteristics of the light so produced can be varied, and some kinds approximate to white light. But the so-called 'daylight' type tends towards blue, which makes red surfaces appear dull, whereas blue and green surfaces appear stronger. Another type, described as 'warm white' tends towards yellow, which makes blue appear grey, and yellow and orange deeper. Either of these types, used exclusively, is psychologically unsatisfactory, and sometimes the two are mixed to obtain a more acceptable light.
3. *Mercury and sodium discharge lamps*, which are types much used for illuminating roads and open spaces. Both produce light that is markedly deficient in part of the spectrum, so that coloured surfaces bear little resemblance to their daylight appearance.

   Mercury lamps, although improved, are still inclined to blue-green, with consequent distortion of other colours – and the human complexion!

   Sodium lamps, which are also used for the floodlighting of buildings, produce a strong yellow light having similar effects; reds, for example, look muddy brown.

The foregoing indicates the importance of studying various types of artificial lights and their effects, and emphasises that it is not only necessary that adequate illumination is provided for practical purposes in urban areas, but that the light falling on the surfaces of roads, pavings, buildings and landscape will not be visually unpleasant, but will contribute positively to the design.

Colour

For practical purposes, it is usual to describe colour in three dimensions: hue, value or tone, and intensity.

1. HUE distinguishes one colour from another, e.g. yellow, blue, red, etc. There are three basic hues, which are the primary colours red, blue and yellow. From these, any number of intermediate hues can be obtained by mixing in various combinations and proportions. This can be expressed by means of a colour circle, but only effectively for a relatively small number of colours.
2. VALUE or TONE is the relative lightness or darkness of a colour. A light (in the value sense) colour will reflect more light (in the real

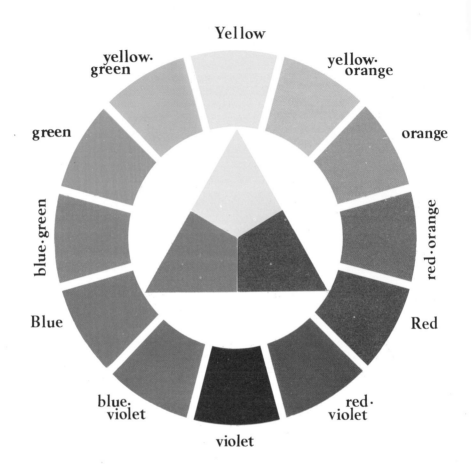

Yellow

yellow·green

green

blue·green

Blue

blue·violet

violet

red·violet

Red

red·orange

orange

yellow·orange

PRIMARY COLOURS and
COLOUR CIRCLE (12 hues)

HEAVY MOBILE
EQUIPMENT
AND PLANT, ETC.

TRAFFIC
SIGNALS

TRAFFIC SIGNS

Stamford A 1

Huntingdon
A 141

DIRECTION SIGNS

RADIO MASTS
ETC. NEAR
AIRPORTS

DISTINCTIVE COLOURS
FOR WARNINGS

sense) than a dark colour, although both may be the same hue. Reference to a colour wheel shows that some hues are lighter than others, e.g. yellow is lighter than blue. It is not possible to have a really dark yellow.

3. INTENSITY describes the purity or strength of a hue ranging from neutral grey to the purest and strongest version of the hue as derived from white light.

From these dimensions, it is possible by using scales based thereon, i.e. numerical graduations, to give a scientific measurement to any colour sensation. Instead of trying to describe colours by subjective and arbitrary names like: 'forest green', 'wedgwood blue', 'beige', etc., which can be variously interpreted and so lead to confusion, letters and numerals can give precise descriptions, which are always the same, whether applied to a painted surface, or to a textile, or a ceramic, when reflecting from white light. Thus, a standard range of colours can be established.

The system of colour classification most commonly used, and which is based on the foregoing dimensions, is the Munsell system, named after the American art teacher who produced it. This system, with some modifications, is used for standardising colours in the construction and manufacturing industries, and these standard colours are normally used by designers.*

In environmental design and the design of buildings, colours are not considered in isolation. Every colour impression or sensation is affected by adjoining and adjacent colours and by the total effect of its surroundings and background. In this connection, important factors are *HARMONY* and *CONTRAST*. So far as hue is concerned, harmonious colours are those which are closely related, so that, used together, they give a feeling of unity and coherence with associated psychological reactions of security and relaxation. Closeness of tones or values in the use of such hues reinforces the effect. Contrasting colours, on the other hand, are hues which are opposite one another on the colour circle, e.g. green and red. They are known as complementary colours. The placing of such colours together or in juxtaposition intensifies them. Contrasting colours are used to add visual 'interest', to brighten a design, where such an effect is appropriate, to draw attention to a particular feature, to emphasise an element of importance, e.g. an entrance. Generally, in urban design large surface areas, horizontal and vertical, are in harmonious colours and with such details and incidental items in contrasting colours. Hue is not the only consideration. Contrast of value or tone and of intensity can be employed to reinforce the effect. Main

* British Standards Institution DD17 'Basic range for the co-ordination of colours for building purposes.'

areas are usually of low reflective value tending towards the neutral end of the scale of intensity, whereas particular elements of interest are bright and pure in colour.

Examples of simple contrasting colours for the purpose of attracting attention or giving definition are : the alternate red and white painting of radio-masts and other obstructions in the vicinity of airports, so that they are readily visible from the air in contrast to the green of grass or the darker colours of pavings and buildings; the black and white banding of light-houses, pedestrian-crossings, road barriers, etc., the yellow and black diagonal stripes on heavy mobile earth-moving equipment, etc.

The strongest contrast in the case of signs, i.e. most visible at a distance, is that of black letters on a yellow ground. However, all circumstances have to be considered in selecting colours, such as positions of viewpoints, nature of background, existing near-by colours, and so on. Instances have occurred of accidents resulting from confusion between traffic signals and adjacent coloured advertisements. The effect of artificial lighting which may change the appearance of colours must not be overlooked.

General use of colour. As it is by means of light, which is composed of colours, that the environment is perceived, then the conscious use of colours, both in the selection of materials and the application of pigments, must be related to surfaces ; properly used, colours should aid the recognition and appreciation of form and make clear spatial arrangements. The opposite of this : the use of colours regardless of forms and shapes, the deliberate creation of visual confusion, i.e. camouflage, is disturbing and perplexing to the eye and the mind. Where there should be distinction and certainty, there is lack of definition and so doubt.

Psychological effects of colours. Colours affect people emotionally. While such mental reactions are individual and subjective, there is evidence that, in general, certain colours are likely to produce certain feelings, and this aspect should receive consideration in regard to external design as well as interior design, where it is of great importance because of the more intimate relationship with people, and the finer degree to which it can be controlled.

Examples of generally accepted colour response are :

BLUE — soothing effect, if not too strong; but excess of deep blue is depressing (the 'blues' !) ; not suitable for extensive use externally.

GREEN — similar in effect to blue ; not suitable where seen together with natural greens, i.e. grass, foliage, etc.

YELLOW — cheering and stimulating ; attractive in the sense of drawing attention ; also commonly recognised as a warning sign.

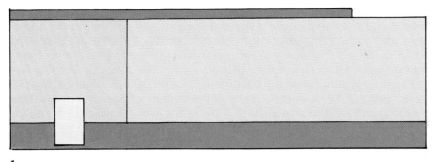

harmony

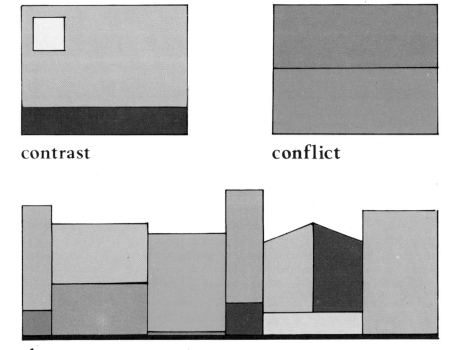

contrast   conflict

chaos

EXTERIOR COLOURS

Sunlight on
cumulus clouds
over Wiltshire
Downs, England,
(below) another
example of white
light. Patches of
blue sky are caused
by midday
atmospheric
absorption of other
colours. Moving
cloud shadows add
interest to the
harmonious colours
of trees, grass and
crops.

Wind blown water
jets in the central
area pool of
Tapiola New Town,
Finland, show the
rainbow effect of
spray breaking
sunlight into its
constituent colours.

RED – exciting; in combination with red and white, friendly; but not suitable for extensive use except pale or subdued tones; in small, strong areas, widely recognised as a sign for danger.

PURPLE – in small areas, richness and importance; in large areas, disturbing.

BROWNS – restful and comforting, especially in combination with orange and yellow, and some gold or white.

GREYS – if tending towards blue, depressing unless combined with livelier colour, but if tending towards brown, and light in tone are pleasing and satisfying.

WHITE – cheering and stimulating, especially when reflecting sunlight, and in combination with bright primary colour accents.

Black is for various technical reasons unsuitable for large areas; when so used, because of the reflective value of the materials, it is really a deep grey. However, both black and white in small areas and strips, which appear more intense, are valuable means of providing accents to and of separating areas of other colours for improved visual definition and perception.

We turn now to 'warm' and 'cool' colours, and the phenomena known as 'spatial effect of colour'. Chromatic variation causes the eye to refocus for different colours; this creates the illusion that warm colours, e.g. yellow and red, advance and that cool colours recede. This effect is increased by tone: strong colours advance; pale colours recede. However, dark blue and black, which might be expected to advance, actually appear to recede, possibly because of association with the night sky and 'tunnel' effects. The general principle remains that the colours of major areas or roads, pavings, walls and roofs, are best in more or less neutral, although not negative hues, with bright, intense colours used for small accented features. Regard must be paid to location, background, climatic and atmospheric conditions (tropical, temperate and far north), amounts of sunshine, rainfall and snow. Light-coloured pavings in the tropics might cause unpleasant glare.

Colours should always be compatible in the urban scene. Garish combinations of primary hues should not be permitted outside fairs and light entertainment centres: firstly, because although initially arresting and perhaps exciting, the novelty wears off quickly, and inevitable weathering reduces impact so that the effect becomes irritating and even sordid in a short time, while quieter colours remain unchanged in visual appeal; secondly, there is the paradox that, in temperate climes with many overcast days, such colours, instead of brightening the scene, actually have a depressing effect.

4
Surfaces

The previous chapter dealt with the perception of surfaces in nature and in man-made structures as areas of colour. This chapter extends consideration of perception to texture, pattern, and light and shade. These qualities of what is seen are all perceived together with colour, but in dealing with them separately, they can be better understood, and their effects and uses in visual design better appreciated.

Texture

Texture modifies colour. If two surfaces are both of the same hue and intensity, but are of different textures, they will not look alike. Texture can be regarded as the impression through sight of what can be experienced by touch. Indeed, the same words, e.g. ROUGH, SMOOTH, etc. are used to describe texture whether a surface is seen or felt.

The texture of a surface can be inherent in the nature of the material, as with the bark of a tree, rock face, animal skin; or can result from manufacture, as in the cases of brick, concrete, wrought metals, woods and plastics, or it can be imposed by plastering, painting, chipping and grooving. It can also be simulated on smooth surfaces by photographic processes.

The relative degree of fineness or coarseness of texture is normally judged by the naked eye at fairly close proximity under average conditions of lighting, but distance is a factor that has to be taken into account in design, particularly in regard to groups of buildings and urban compositions generally. Distance tends to diminish surface texture. What appears rough at short range appears smooth or smoother when viewed from afar.

Another factor affecting appearance is the strength and direction of the light that falls upon and is reflected by the surface. A rough surface illuminated directly by a strong light from behind the spectator, will seem smoother than when seen from the same point with the light shining from

Detail (above) of rough, exposed aggregate, precast concrete panels of building (right) contrasted with smooth, fair-face, concrete units forming window surrounds. Projection of latter provides interesting shade and shadow effects which emphasise the facade pattern.

the side. This is because the side light causes a more pronounced effect of shadow and shade, which are described later in this chapter.

Texture, then, varies in the same way as do hue and intensity of colour as the light changes in position and strength – movement of the sun in varying atmospheric conditions – and as the spectator changes position and views the surfaces from different angles and at different distances. Consideration has therefore to be given in design to the possibilities and probable results in these respects in regard to the orientation of the surfaces and to both natural and artificial lighting.

The following are suggested as principles or guide-lines for the use and the appreciation of texture:

1. If possible, and it usually is, the texture of surfaces should result from the selection of those materials that are suitable primarily for functional and constructional purposes. A particular texture may be required for practical reasons, e.g. a smooth surface is more easily cleaned, or for a particular expression of character, e.g. rough surface may indicate strength or security.
2. A texture should not be applied as a veneer unless there are strong and compelling reasons. It may be necessary sometimes to resort to a cosmetic treatment, when the basic structure is unavoidably poor in appearance or has deteriorated because of age and neglect.
3. In urban design, there should be textural unity in a building or in a group of associated buildings. This does not necessarily mean uniformity, but that there should be a dominant texture, which is the key to the character of the composition. There should not be too many different and conflicting textures. Contrast of textures, as of colours, can be used appropriately to give interest but violently diverse and competing areas of texture produces a restless and divisive effect. This is a common fault in much urban and building design. For example, a shiny corrugated aluminium roof covering on a cottage of traditional design with masonry walls, is both functionally and structurally satisfactory, but, by reason of the difference in texture, it is visually offensive. Similarly, a metal and glass multi-storey city office building may well have a constrasting area of walling at the ground storey, but surely not rustic brickwork or stuck-on thin slabs of random river stone when panels of polished granite or of ceramic would be far more satisfactory and compatible in texture.

Transparent, translucent and reflective surfaces

As well as normal textured surfaces, consideration has to be given to surfaces which are transparent, translucent or highly reflective, in environ-

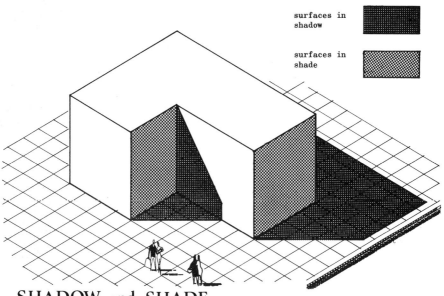

surfaces in shadow

surfaces in shade

SHADOW and SHADE

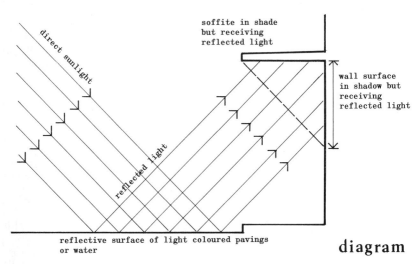

direct sunlight

soffite in shade but receiving reflected light

wall surface in shadow but receiving reflected light

reflected light

reflective surface of light coloured pavings or water

diagram

REFLECTED LIGHT

mental design. Many types of buildings have external walls or envelopes consisting of large areas of clear glass. In some cases, this is to enable the occupants to see out extensively; in others, it is to enable those outside to look in. Shop and showroom windows are examples of the latter, but it is not unusual for banks, bottling and mechanical plants, etc. to be similarly provided. With these buildings, what is seen inside becomes part of their overall appearance, and the relationship of external and internal design, as seen both by day and night, must be carefully integrated.

Then there are buildings which, for one reason or another, have façade panels of obscure glass or translucent plastic. Such panels are often illuminated from behind, and various visual effects can be obtained. These effects, too, must be considered in relation to other materials in the same building to ensure compatibility, and the materials and character of adjoining buildings and immediate surroundings in order to avoid visual conflict.

As regards highly reflective materials, which throw back almost total light, e.g. mirror glass, polished metals and certain kinds of plastics, while they have qualities of brilliance and sparkle, thus providing means of imparting 'life' and enrichment, they, in particular, should be employed with discretion. If used in excess, they not only cause annoying glare in sunlight, but the reflections of sky and clouds, other buildings and moving vehicles can be visually disturbing. As attention-grabbing devices they are obnoxious and have no place in civilised urban design, except in amusement centres as daytime counterparts to nocturnal illuminated signs and flashing lights.

Shadows and shade

Shadows and shade enable the eye to define form and to perceive the relationships between various surfaces.

A surface in shadow is one that receives no direct light from the main light source because something prevents the light rays reaching it. A surface in shade is one that receives no direct light or diminished light from the main light source because it is facing away from it wholly or in part.

During daytime, the main outside light source is the sun. At night, apart from moonlight and starlight, which are usually too weak to be of consequence, light on buildings, roads and open spaces comes from artificial sources, such as street lamps, floodlights or light shining out from other buildings.

Daylight varies in direction as the earth revolves, and as the seasons change, and in intensity from dawn through noon to dusk. It is further modified by transient atmospheric conditions, and it differs in strength according to geographical location. Night lighting is almost always from fixed points and is generally consistent, although affected by the weather.

Low-angled sunlight emphasises building form and surface textures, showing contrast between smooth moulded glass-reinforced-plastic panels and rough split concrete block facings. Note variety of facade patterns with geometrical integration of all elements.

Serrated form of repeated plan units of nurses' hostel casts characteristic shadows. Note contrast of colour tone and of textures between upper and lower parts of building.

Example of building (right) with highly reflective — glass and steel — external surface which, in bright sunlight, can impart brilliance and 'life' to the urban scene, but used indiscriminately or in tropical areas may cause glare and dazzle.

Typical, fully-glazed shop front (below) giving clear view of well-arranged interior by day; and at night, when the illuminated lettering and symbol — of excellent design — are equally effectively displayed.

Therefore, although there are some considerable variables, shadows and shades, whether sharp or diffused, resulting from particular forms or arrangements of masses and detail can be estimated if not precisely calculated and they also are factors to be taken into account in the design process. Firstly, they have to be considered in relation to form, texture and pattern. Secondly, there are practical considerations, such as the avoidance of dark or dim areas for reasons of safety and security, and the prevention of confusing and therefore dangerous shadows which mislead the eye, such as shadows across steps. Thirdly, there are psychological considerations – in the Northern Hemisphere, for example, the north-facing side of a shopping street is less favoured by shoppers, presumably because, receiving little sun, it is comparatively less attractive. Conversely, in the tropics, shade provides relief from sun and glare, and this has manifest advantages psychologically and physically, as described in a later chapter.

For these considerations, those most directly concerned with the design of buildings and of the environment, show conventional shadows and shades on sketch schemes and drawings, as described in the author's book *Draughtsmanship,** and models made for the study of development projects are photographed, not only from different angles but with lighting from different points to give approximations of what actual shadows and shades will result when the designs are implemented.

Where sunshine can be relied upon, particular advantage can be taken of elements such as balconies or canopies as means of providing interest to building façades and to building masses.

Few primary shadows and shades have absolute values. Complex reflected light rays cause infinite gradations of back shadows and shades, which fortuitously enliven the scene by day; this effect also occurs from the intersections and reflections from multi-light sources in towns at night. Similar effects can be made use of in conscious design in tropical and subtropical regions, or wherever the sun is sufficiently strong, by providing reflective horizontal surfaces or pools of water – the latter having the added advantage of giving 'dancing' reflections – which throw light upwards on to related soffites and wall surfaces.

Floodlighting from low level reverses the normal or downward direction of daylighting and, while the effects can be dramatic, the design qualities of older stylistic buildings can be denigrated or even destroyed unless care is exercised. New buildings intended to be floodlit are designed accordingly.

Pattern is another word of several meanings, and it is sometimes confused with texture. But in the senses the words are used here, texture is a visually perceived tactile condition and pattern is the regular repetition of an arrangement of lines, shapes and/or areas of colour.

* Second edition published 1969 by Edward Arnold.

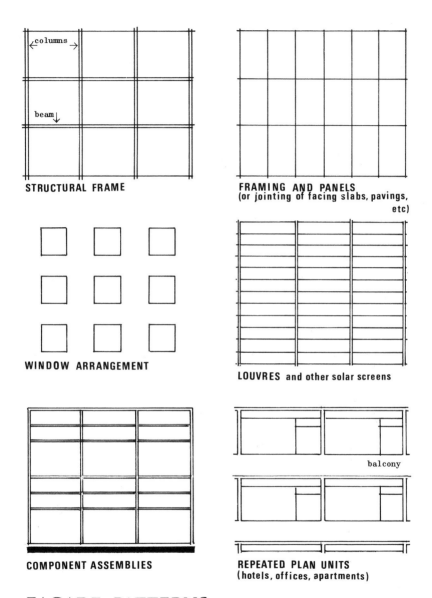

STRUCTURAL FRAME

FRAMING AND PANELS
(or jointing of facing slabs, pavings,
etc)

WINDOW ARRANGEMENT

LOUVRES and other solar screens

COMPONENT ASSEMBLIES

REPEATED PLAN UNITS
(hotels, offices, apartments)

balcony

FACADE PATTERNS
examples of derivations

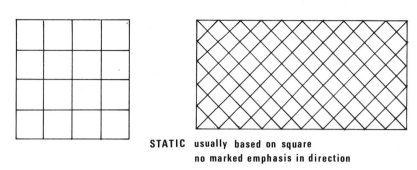

STATIC usually based on square
no marked emphasis in direction

HORIZONTAL

VERTICAL

DIRECTION

Generally, emphasis
follows shape, eg.
facade pattern of
tall building is
'vertical' in direction,
but closely spaced
regular bands can
be used contrary to
shape on relatively
long, low facades or
narrow, high towers

HORIZONTAL

VERTICAL

FACADE PATTERNS   basic visual effects

In urban and building design, the basis of pattern is usually a rectangular grid, although it can be any simple geometrical figure, and patterns can occur on any surface of sufficient relative size to accommodate a reasonable number of repetitions. It does not matter whether the surface is horizontal, vertical, inclined or curved.

Pattern can result from the ways materials are used, e.g. the bonding of brickwork, the joint lines of facings or pavings, etc., or it may arise from the elements of functional or structural design, such as the arrangement of openings, framing and panels, or the intersection of the vertical lines of supporting columns, i.e. bay divisions, by the horizontal lines of floor levels, with subsidiary lines of mullions, sills, balconies, and all the various recesses and breaks contributing to the general effect. Examples of the latter are buildings composed of standard plan elements: blocks of offices or apartments and large hotels, whereon the pattern extends over almost the whole façade. Similarly, buildings designed and constructed on a modular basis or an industrialised system automatically have façade patterns of this kind. In the tropics, the use of louvres, solar screens and other types of protection from heat and glare also provide interesting external visual patterns.

Façade patterns are of major importance in urban design as their visual effect is considerable, as referred to in the following chapters, and compatibility of patterns of adjoining and adjacent buildings and other structures is essential.

Although elevational design should derive from and should honestly express plan function and structure, some reciprocal adjustment is usually possible, and façade patterns can be further legitimately modified by stressing some elements and subduing others, by the selection and manipulation of materials, colours and textures to achieve not only the visually satisfactory design of an individual building but also of the building in relation to its neighbours and surroundings.

A façade pattern can be static or directional. A static pattern has a balance of horizontal and vertical elements and the eye is not drawn one way or the other. This has a restful effect and can be used to avoid competition with other buildings or landscape, and preferably where there is a strong point of interest elsewhere, to which the façade is acting as a background. Without such an interest, however, extensive static façades can be dull. A directional pattern is one that has definite emphasis either horizontally or vertically, and the eye tends to move accordingly. Emphasis can be obtained by stressing lines or features, often by connecting windows in bands either along or up and down the façade.

It is generally held that tall buildings should have vertical emphasis and long, low buildings should have horizontal emphasis, otherwise there is conflict between the direction of the pattern and the overall shape of the façade. This is especially so where the effect is of alternate light (wall) and

Multi-storey office buildings (above) with simple rectangular facade patterns resulting from stressed structural verticals in combination with horizontal bands of windows.

Tower building (left) with each upper storey strongly defined horizontally by continuous windows with plain, light-coloured facings between, by the overall visual direction is vertical. The foreground paving pattern reflects the light and dark strips of the building.

FACADE PATTERN Examples

Interesting pattern of structurally derived diagonals superimposed on broad horizontal bands at each floor level in car parking building (below). Visual direction is appropriately horizontal. Relationship between diagonal units and V supports of the building contributes to the unity of the design.

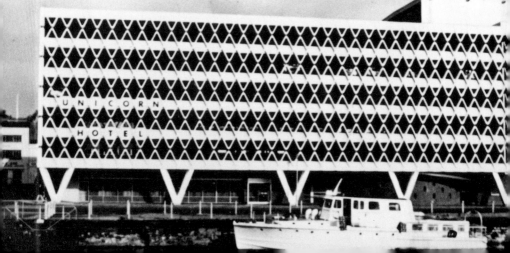

FACADE PATTERN

Example of regular pattern of hotel facade resulting from repeated plan elements — the guest rooms.

Air view (above) showing main facades.

Detail (right) of balconies to guest rooms.

dark (windows) bands, as vertical bands tend to increase the appearance of height, and horizontal bands the appearance of width. But there are exceptions. If the alternate horizontal bands are even and regular on a high building, in other words, if, as it were, there is a pile of them, they read together in a vertical direction and the visual effect can be satisfactory. It may indeed be better than vertical banding, which might over-dramatise the design in relation to neighbouring structures or surroundings. What is widely accepted, however, is that a directional pattern should be positive. The unsatisfactory appearance of many otherwise well-designed buildings will be found, on examination, to be due to weakness in this respect.

Both horizontal and vertical emphasis may be found in parts of one building or in different buildings of a group; if so, one direction should be clearly dominant, and set the key for the composition.

Wall surfaces which may occur at the ends of buildings or elsewhere to contain services, lifts and the like, where there is no functional or structural reason to provide openings or other features, these surfaces are best left blank. They can be provided with attractive and durable finish, rather than waste money on applying some arbitrary pattern that soon becomes boring, and which diminishes the value of the wall as a contrast to fenestrated and patterned areas. Such blank walls are often of value for lettering or the placing of symbols, flag-poles, etc.

Where a pattern is imposed and does not come about logically from functional or structural expression or from the constructional materials used, but is applied to add interest, a guiding principle is that the pattern, what-ever its kind, should visually reinforce the shape or form of the surface concerned. The repetitive unit should be related mathematically to the dimensions of the area; in short, it should fit the space available. A large unit pattern, unless part of a larger scheme, should not be used on a small area although the distance from where the pattern is normally viewed has to be taken into account. Care must be taken with the meeting of patterned surfaces at corners and with other elements in the same plane to avoid awkwardnesses and 'near misses' at junctions.

Where the pattern is pictorial, as opposed to a purely abstract arrange-ment of lines, or reliefs – although with these, too, the principle has relevance – it should have some significance in relation to the building or its situation. The pattern should not be merely a stock-piece of banal decoration.

5
Form, Shape and Line

Form

Colour, texture and pattern refer to surfaces, but buildings and other structures are perceived also as forms, shapes and lines. For clarity, the word 'form' is used here in a three-dimensional sense; 'shape' in a two-dimensional sense; and 'lines' means outlines, edges, junctions of surfaces, joints, and any long thin projections and recesses.

The forms of buildings, structures and all designed objects are basically derived from function and construction or manufacture. Such forms, when definite and not obscured, are described as functional or structural expression. It would seem to be a not unreasonable principle of design that this expression in form of function or construction should be clear and unequivocal. The expression need not be crude – there are other factors affecting form – but it is best if it is simple, as there is little doubt that the objective eye prefers and is most satisfied by readily apprehensible forms than those that are visually untidy and complex. Most buildings and civil engineering works do, in fact, have the appearance of geometrical solids or combinations of such solids, e.g. rectangular blocks, cubes, pyramids, cones, cylinders, spheres and hemispheres, etc.

However, as well as forms resulting from the efficient enclosing of space for particular purposes and/or from the adoption of a structural system appropriate to the function, the principle factor determining the form may be the needs of the environmental or urban composition of which the buildings or structures will be part. The two aspects, form from within and form from without, do not conflict. Many general kinds of accommodation can be contained in simple rectangular blocks, the precise form of which is not critical; and forms necessary for special buildings can be given suitable individual sites. The urban designer at one and the same time (*a*) locates buildings and other environmental elements with regard to uses and other

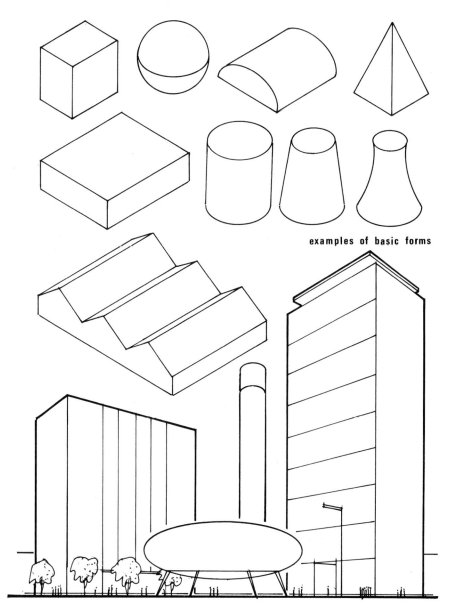

examples of basic forms

FORM geometric examples 3D

FORM

The forms of many buildings are compositions of rectangular blocks arranged horizontally or vertically as illustrated by these three typical examples.

Pyramidal blocks of holiday apartments by marina (above) at La Grande Motte, France.

FORM Examples of Building Form

Part-spherical geodesic domed exhibition building (right) Montreal, Canada. Also example of structural surface pattern.

Nuclear power station at
Oldbury-on-Severn (above),
showing reactor block
containing two reactors,
linked by common service
building and turbine hall
with three gas turbine
chimneys : a variety of forms
including circular forms
emphasised by vertical 'lines'
as well as graded shades.

FORM

Examples of function-
derived forms in power
station design.

Coal-fired power station at
Ironbridge (right) showing
three of the hyperboloid
cooling towers, rectangular
blocks of the turbine hall,
boiler house, etc. and the
high circular chimney.

FORM AND FUNCTION

Water towers, Alençon, France. A superb example of functional design, which also
expresses unequivocally the construction in reinforced concrete. The ribbed surface
texture emphasises the form by light and shade.

considerations and (*b*) determines broadly their overall sizes and forms – allowing some latitude for subsequent modification – within the limits of visual composition.

Attention is given to the psychological effects of different forms and different arrangements of forms and their relationships with surroundings and backgrounds.

Shape

Many varied shapes occur in layouts, e.g. roads, roundabouts, open spaces and building plots, and in buildings, e.g. façades, door and window openings, and also in minor objects and details of all kinds. Some are essentially geometrical: regular figures such as rectangles, squares, circles or triangles; others are more complex consisting of combinations of straight and curved lines; and some are wholly irregular and 'free'. The determination of shapes results almost automatically in the processes of planning and building design, that is the shapes are derived from efficient functional arrangement and economic construction. Manipulation within limits is usually possible, however, and the aim of the designer should be to avoid awkward, ugly and impractical shapes having inappropriate associations. The eye is quick to seize on shapes reminiscent of the shapes of other erections and objects, and to make disparaging comparisons. Each designed shape should be neatly integrated with adjoining shapes without 'left-overs'; a good design is a mosaic of tidy, well-shaped pieces, each contributing smoothly to the overall effect.

Shapes have emotional impact in much the same way as corresponding forms, and can be employed accordingly where a particular psychological response is a part of function. In addition, certain shapes have strong visual effects; squares and circles, to relative small scale, tend to attract and hold the eye and so may be used as focal points or 'stops'; conversely they can be deliberately not used if effect would be undesirable. Long rectangles, as noted in regard to pattern, tend to lead the eye along the direction of their length.

Generally, the more regular and geometric shapes, mostly rectangular, are appropriate to urban layouts and buildings at one end of the range, and freer and curving shapes for landscaping and rural planning at the other.

Line

In all planning and building design there are straight lines: horizontal, vertical and inclined, and curved lines: either parts of circles, ellipses, parabolas or free flowing. Indeed, plans and drawings, design analogues, are mainly composed of lines. They derive from forms and shapes and

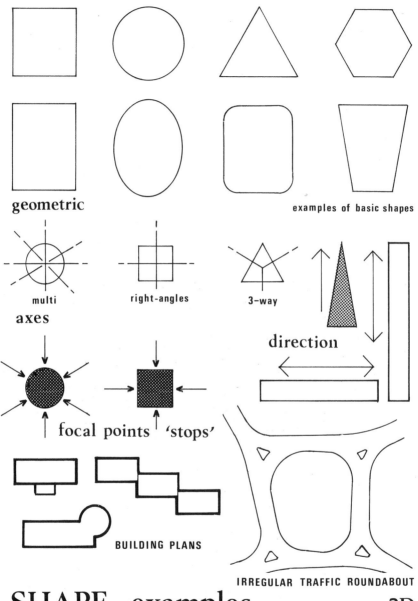

geometric

examples of basic shapes

multi

right-angles

3-way

axes

direction

focal points 'stops'

BUILDING PLANS

IRREGULAR TRAFFIC ROUNDABOUT

SHAPE examples 2D

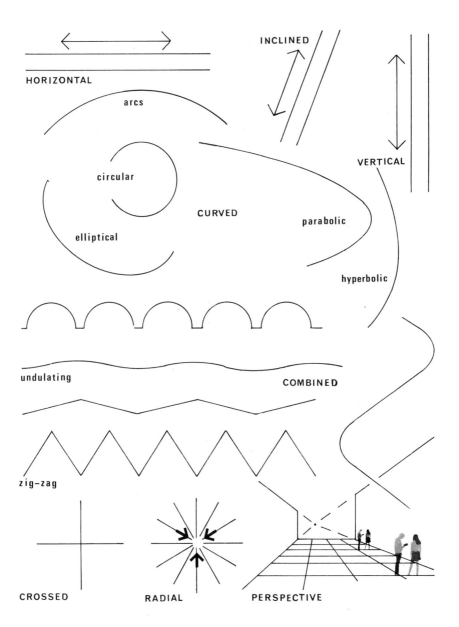

HORIZONTAL

arcs

INCLINED

circular

elliptical

CURVED

parabolic

hyperbolic

VERTICAL

undulating

COMBINED

zig-zag

CROSSED

RADIAL

PERSPECTIVE

LINE examples   1D

jointings. So produced, they can be legitimately strengthened or subdued for improved visual effect, e.g. to define pattern, impart 'direction' and increase textural effect but lines should not be added without genuine functional or structural justification. It is quite wrong, for example, to scratch lines on plaster or concrete surfaces with the object of imitating masonry joints : it deceives no one and the result is as absurd as it is false.

Some of the visual effects of lines are : emphasised horizontal lines on long low buildings or structures is restful to the eye ; stressed vertical lines on tall buildings are stimulating ; inclined lines, unless clearly related to form or construction, can be disturbing but if regularly arranged can help define form : crossed lines produce points of interest at the intersections ; curved lines have a softening effect ; slow regular undulating lines impart rhythm and calmness ; sharply pointed or zigzag lines are restless and perhaps disturbing. These are only a few common examples. Much depends on circumstances. What is important is that the effect of lines must receive consideration together with form and shape in the design process.

Composition

Composition is the conscious arrangement of parts or elements to produce a functionally and visually satisfying whole.

In planning, the parts include buildings and other man-made structures with the paved spaces in and around them, roads and railways, parks and recreation areas, gardens and landscaping. These are elements of land use. In addition there are many items of street furniture and amenity. All should be individually and collectively well designed and well arranged to provide the means for efficient and agreeable living.

The overriding principle to be observed in the arrangement is that of integration, which is that everything is appropriate and belongs to the whole, and that nothing is alien or incongruous.

In urban design, the basis of integrity or unity or homogeneity is the disposition of major plan elements so that there are discernible groupings centred about focal-points of special importance and interest.

The two-dimensional town plan will result from practical considerations of the assessed requirements of land uses and communications, influenced by a multitude of social and economic factors. But its ultimate realisation must be kept in mind from the beginning of and throughout the process of design formulation. That is why it is so important for all concerned to know about the principles of design, and thereby to be able effectively to co-operate towards the final goal.

The location of focal-points is a matter of functional suitability in conjunction with visual emphasis. The two aspects cannot be separated. In the selection of sites, advantage may be taken of topographical and landscape

Simple, rectangular block in form with cornice of narrow projection and shallow frontal recess (expressing banking hall within); much of the interest results from rectilinear pattern of jointings and framings, the arrangements of which are based on mathematical relationships giving strong unity to the composition. Walls are faced with precast slabs of exposed porcelain chip aggregate. Angles of the building and certain verticals, corresponding with structural members, are stressed by use of aluminium sections. Rough texture of wall slabs contrasts with smooth polished black granite plinth, plastic signs, and areas of glass. The general harmonious colours of warm greys and aluminium are foil to black lettering and brightly hued coat of arms and mosaic abstracts along side. Lettering is not only practical, varying in size and style according to positioning and distance from viewpoints, but also constitutes important integrated design elements.

LINE IN DESIGN

Example of a building in which 'lines' in the sense defined in the text establish related shapes, and make a major contribution to the design.

features : hills, lake-sides, bends of rivers, scenic backgrounds. In past ages towns and villages often had a church or castle as a dominant building near which a square or green would be the focal-point. Today, we are more likely to find high commercial buildings or tower blocks of apartments as the visual dominants in existing towns, and the former may be in the central area, although it would be more seemly, as does happen, for the more important civic and public buildings to have the most prominent position.

In extensive urban areas, more than one focal-point may be necessary, arranged centrally as a series of connected centres for commerce, shopping and public transport, with secondary foci for outlying districts. This planned provision of nodes is a usual basis for the layout of new towns or town extensions.

By orientation is meant the location of the various component parts of the town design so that, in conjunction with the communications network, residents and visitors are able to comprehend the layout and to be aware of its coherence, unlike so many sprawling amorphous urban developments of the nineteenth and early twentieth centuries, whose vast areas of un-relieved dullness, endless shop-lined roads, and absence of effective focal-points produce a depressing 'lost' feeling.

Summarising the above comments, a town should have a clearly defined centre where people can gather and where the more important buildings are located, with subsidiary centres as necessary, all interconnected and integrated in a logical and convenient way.

As regard the buildings and other elements of urban design location, size, height and arrangement must be studied in relation to the foregoing. And while the use of compatible materials and colours, with reasonable variety of individual design and judicious contrast for liveliness and interest, are valuable contributors to unity and integrity in the overall design in an urban composition, equally important is the maintaining of harmonious proportions and correct scale.

Proportion

Proportion in visual design refers to the ratio between related distances, lengths or sizes of mass and area. Proportion can be a matter of three dimensions or two.

A rectangular site may have sides in the proportion of 1 : 3 ; that is, it is three times longer than it is wide.

A door opening may be in the proportion of 2 : 1 ; it is twice as high as it is wide. But it could be twice as wide as it is high. Depending upon size and use, either could be satisfactory.

A free-standing building of rectangular block form may be in the proportions of 3 : 2 : 1. So may a matchbox. Whether or not each is of good proportion can only be to the extent its size and shape meet the requirements of function. In present-day design, good proportions are not those imposed by an arbitrary set of 'rules' or pseudo-scientific theory, but are those which result from planning forms and shapes and structural elements. Certainly the eye is pleased by simple geometrical relations, and by the repetition of these relationships in a composition, as described in regard to pattern in the previous chapter.

Mathematical and geometrical design theories

In discussing proportion and scale, some mention must be made of mathematical and geometrical design theories. Since the days of Ancient Greece, and possibly before, there has been something of primitive superstition about the subject, and various theories have been put forward to try to show that good or perfect design has a mathematical basis of a fairly simple nature that has been used unconsciously, presumably, by inspired designers of the past and which can be applied by the cognoscenti of the present. A parallel has been drawn with musical composition, which is certainly based on mathematical proportions in the aural sense, and this has been summarised in the rather idiotic phrase 'architecture is frozen music'! In fact there is very little in common with other arts, architecture being a good deal more than an art, and to pursue the parallel is profitless. Indeed, there is little practical value in any of the theories, which can only be utilised with great difficulty if at all in the complex structures of the present day.

The theories are by no means consistent and sometimes contradictory. There is an element of truth in them but their principal fascination lies in the mystical attributes which causes those who are otherwise quite rational to be carried away by them.

Alas ! good design is not so magically to be achieved. As earlier chapters have explained it is the result of a logical process not an abracadabra of figures and shapes and lines, but facts, knowledge, principles, with some imagination and a lot of hard thinking.

The element of truth is that the eye and mind are pleased and satisfied by the appearance of designs of all kinds in which clear mathematical ratios occur and which are composed of simple geometrical forms, and in which there may be a repetition of shapes and dimensions. In other words, where there is a mathematical relationship between the various parts of a composition, whether a single building or a large environmental layout, an important means of obtaining that essential coherence, referred to earlier in this chapter, will result. The designer should make use of this recognised human trait in the conception, development and refinement of his projects, but to dogmatise about certain proportions or to postulate 'rules', is as presumptuous as it is worthless.

This brings us to buildings designed in accordance with dimensional co-ordination, which can be described as 'organising dimensions so as to reduce the variety of sizes to which components have to be made; and also to enable components to be used together on the job without modification.' In other words: the construction of buildings from factory-produced standard components, the sizes of which enable them to be fitted together on site without cutting or shaping.

Further reference to this is made in a later chapter, but the point to be brought out here is that the adoption of a modular system – a module being a basic dimension of which all other dimensions are multiples – automatically produces mathematical relationships between the parts of the buildings so designed and therefore goes some way towards achieving visual satisfaction in that respect. The visual aspect of design is incidental: the object of dimension co-ordination is to obtain maximum economy from the use of mass-production of the minimum number of components and speed of erection, but there is, at least, a basis for good appearance provided judgement is made in accordance with fundamental principles free from preconceptions and prejudice arising from other methods of building.

Similarly, any building or any layout which is set out on a grid for reasons of rational space organisation or the economic use of structural framing will possess inherent mathematical relationships which, unless deliberately masked or obscured by disparate outer cladding, must express themselves to the spectator. While the actual dimensions of the grid and any subdivisions are likely within narrow limits to be predetermined by practical or structural requirements, nevertheless the designer will usually have some measure of control exercisable in the initial selection and later adjustments, to modify proportions without losing mathematical relationships.

Mathematical relationships contribute even more greatly to visual effect in other types of structures, e.g. geodesic domes, shell forms, hyperbolic paraboloids, etc., the forms, shapes and details of which are derived from components or forms arranged for structural reasons in regular geometric patterns.

Scale

In town-planning and building design, scale is a word used in connection with the comparison of sizes – mass, area, distance and details – in relation to other normally recognised and accepted sizes. As both are primarily concerned with the needs and activities of humans, the standards are mostly those derived from anthropometrics and ergonomics. A design

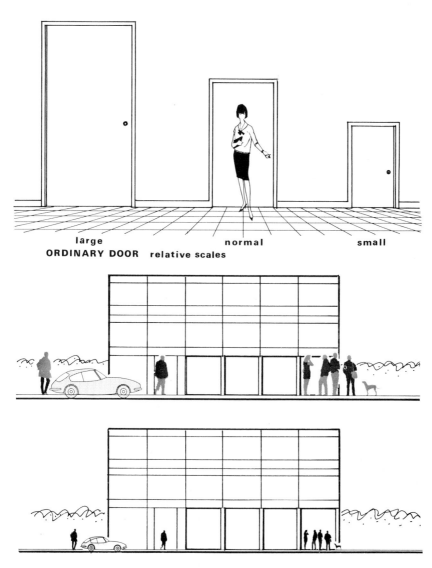

large   normal   small
ORDINARY DOOR relative scales

DIAGRAMMATIC BUILDINGS
IN RELATION FIGURES TO
SHOW COMPARATIVE SIZES

SCALE

or part of a design can therefore be described as 'in scale' if it conforms to human norms, or as 'large in scale' or 'small in scale' according to its departure from those norms.

A doorway in an ordinary small house, intended conveniently to allow the passage of an adult person and household furniture may be 2100 × 900 mm, a size which is reasonably adequate for those uses and which can be described as 'normal scale', but if the doorway is only 1400 × 600 mm, although the proportions remain the same, it is much too small for its purpose and is therefore 'small in scale', or if it is 2800 × 1200 mm, it is far too big and is 'large in scale'. In this example, the doorways that are 'out of scale' will look wrong if not ridiculous in their context, and a designer could hardly make mistakes of that kind.

However, in other situations, errors in scale are not so readily discernible during the design process, and the inexperienced designer in whatever field, must be continually on the alert to avoid 'loss of scale'. Studies of examples of the past and critical examination of recent and contemporary work of all kinds are helpful in this respect.

Buildings that are often cited as historical examples of largeness of scale are St. Peter's Church in Rome and the unfinished Casa del Diabolo in Vicenza, both of which are compositions of 'correctly' proportioned classical elements, but which have these elements at sizes well beyond the range of dimensions normally associated with them, so that, paradoxically, the buildings would appear much smaller than they actually are, were it not for the presence of people and scale-giving details such as steps.

It is not unreasonable that buildings of public importance should be somewhat larger in scale than normal for visual expression of their character, but the compositions should include elements that enable this over-scale to be appreciated so that the eye is not deceived.

Certainly, smallness of scale has no merit, except for children's playhouses and the toilet fittings in infants' schools! Buildings, which from a distance and seen in isolation, appear in good scale, but which, when closely approached and their true sizes in relation to normal standards becomes manifest, are found to be smaller than first supposed, become visually disappointing and mean, notwithstanding any other qualities of planning and construction which they may possess.

In urban design, problems of scale arise not only in regard to the laying out of buildings and open spaces to keep them within the bounds of human limitations and potentialities – which may in certain cases be extended to include mechanical means of transport – but also in regard to the juxtaposition of buildings and other structures, the scales of which are so dissimilar as to produce discordant and objectionable visual effects. This can happen when various buildings in a new development are separately designed without co-ordinating controls. The solution is not necessarily to

SCALE AND PROPORTION

Lack of related proportions illustrated by adjoining buildings (right), which apart from small old structure, were erected within a few years of one another. Although the heads and sills of the windows of two of the buildings line through, the difference in unit widths causes the narrower facade to appear laterally crushed. The effect of the tall building is mitigated by it being set back and partially separated from its neighbours.

Typical chaotic and visually unsatisfactory urban street scene. (below) Buildings are unrelated in scale, directional pattern, colours, materials and textures.

impose a standard façade, but to require that a satisfactory relationship exists between them, including a scale common to them all.

Incompatibility of scale may also occur when a new building is placed next to a building of a past period, which is being preserved because of its historic or architectural value. There is no reason why the new building should conform in design with the existing, except in cases of infill, but it should either agree in scale or a definite break or gap should be arranged to isolate the older building which is thereby set apart for individual display.

Anthropomorphism

Anthropomorphism in architecture and planning is the identification of human personality characteristics with buildings and the urban scene. For design purposes, it is the consideration of psychological reactions, and how they may be produced by the siting, laying out, massing and grouping of structures and associated landscaping. In the general sense, it is the creation of 'atmosphere', which may be that of an entire town, a village or of an area of development.

Not everyone is equally sensitive to atmosphere, and individual responses vary, yet there is broad agreement as to what is appropriate in particular circumstances. It is beyond the scope of this book to go into this subject in detail, although mention is made of it from time to time. It is sufficient to illustrate its significance by referring to such comparisons as : the difference of atmosphere that should be achieved by physical design between, say, a holiday resort and a manufacturing town, between a civic centre and enclave of private homes, or between a school and a nuclear power station.

6
Functional Planning

Previous chapters have dealt mainly with aspects of visual design but the factor of function was continually stressed. Function is basic to visual design. Consideration is now given to this factor. Until functional requirements are understood and assessed, if only approximately or imperfectly, the rest of the design process is without meaning.

Functional planning

Planning, it is often said, is for people. And with people a start must be made.

People are individual men, women and children, but, although the importance of the individual cannot be over-emphasised, it is those individuals collectively that are the chief concern of planning. People form various, sometimes overlapping and sometimes conflicting, social groups and organisations: national, regional, rural, urban, families, schools, work teams, etc., in all their complexities of strata: political, religious, financial. It is seldom that design is specifically for a single person, e.g. an isolated private dwelling; usually, functional requirements are determined by, or should be determined by the needs, the interests, and the wishes of the social group or groups intimately concerned.

The ascertaining of these requirements is not easy, but it is an essential part of the planning process and, as mentioned earlier, one in which several specialists: sociologists, economists, statisticians and others, contribute information and ideas. Public participation is also a very necessary part of the work at this stage. Information and forecasts have to be compiled, analysed, evaluated and perhaps given priorities in regard to time and money available. The feeding back of experience gained enters into the process.

Problems and difficulties arise from: the existence and persistence of inherited works of the past; inaccuracies of surveys and research (sometimes too crude, sometimes over-sophisticated) ; misdirection of information because of political or other pressures; delays in making surveys, carrying out research, and analysing results which when produced may then be out-of-date; and most of all from changing ideas. The overall planning situation is necessarily fluid in a learning society, as it reflects developments in political, economic, and community concepts, but in regard to the design of the environment, fundamental functional requirements relative to human individuals, must always be:

1. Physical and practical
2. Psychological and emotional

which include:

1. Physical
   (a) Basic needs – shelter (food and clothing), sunlight and air, pure water, sanitation, exercise;
   (b) organisation and controls to implement (a) and to provide employment, education, etc;
   (c) means of transport and communication.

2. Psychological
   (a) personal security, freedom and comfort – freedom from noise and other pollutions; from ugliness, disturbance and disorder;
   (b) community life – opportunities for social and cultural interaction, religious observance, political activity;
   (c) recreation and leisure – access to open spaces, the countryside and seaside; the enjoyment of nature.

These general indications overlap and inter-relate. Physical and psychological requirements can never be wholly separated. The following notes, however, deal with aspects of human physical capabilities and limitations.

Anthropometrics and Ergonomics

The study of human dimensions: sizes, weights and ranges of movements is anthropometry and the resultant data, anthropometrics, extended into the field of ergonomics, provides basic design criteria for the planner as well as for the building designer.

Anthropometric dimensions can be (1) static – those of the standing, sitting or lying figure, and (2) dynamic – movement postures. Methods of obtaining dimensions are fairly well standardised, and diagrams and tables, based on averages and limits of variations, with tolerances, covering most situations are readily available. It is considered acceptable if the requirements of 90–95% of the population or of the category of persons are satisfied. In some cases, a higher percentage is necessary and the higher or lower limit may then become a key factor. Sets of figures for young children, the elderly and infirm, and the handicapped can be applied where appropriate.

Ergonomics is the name given to the scientific study of the relationship between humans and their working environments, which in this sense of the word is taken to include not only physical surroundings but also tools and materials, and work organisation and methods, with the object of increasing efficiency. Ergonomics goes beyond anthropometrics in that it involves behavioural psychology and other disciplines and technologies.

Anthropometric and ergonomic data are particularly the concern of the designer of buildings, e.g. in calculating sizes and shapes of spaces (rooms), corridors or stairs, but it is also essential to the physical planner in regard to the design of footways, pedestrian bridges and subways, railings, location of signs and so on. Consider as examples: *steps* – these occur in many kinds of layouts and have to be designed so that people can raise themselves from one level to another by muscular effort; therefore dimensional limitations are imposed by the physical capabilities of the majority of those who will be using them. However, quite a wide range of proportions of treads to risers fall within those limitations, and a final decision has to be reached taking into account particular purposes of the steps. For example, short flights of broad 'monumental' steps for ease of unhurried negotiation in say a public garden layout or on the approach to an important building will have wide treads and low risers, whereas steps to a subway for the more active pedestrians with no time to lose – ramps being provided for the young, elderly and handicapped – will have relatively narrow treads and high risers in longer flights.

There are desirable ratios between treads and risers; generally, the shorter the one the lower the other, and there are limits according to circumstances to the number of steps in one flight, and minimum widths of landings. Such formulae and recommendations are given in data books, and are sometimes prescribed by building regulations. But they arise in the first instance from human capabilities and behaviour. Similarly, data in respect of pedestrian ramps, i.e. slope, length, width, minimum landings, handrails; heights of guard-rails; widths of footways according to traffic; pedestrian bridge widths and clearances, and dimensions for subways, are other instances where data has been derived from human measurements and design criteria thus obtained.

Mention may be made of walking distances, which are important considerations in residential layouts, e.g. from home to primary school; from house to public transport; from parking point to furthest house for refuse

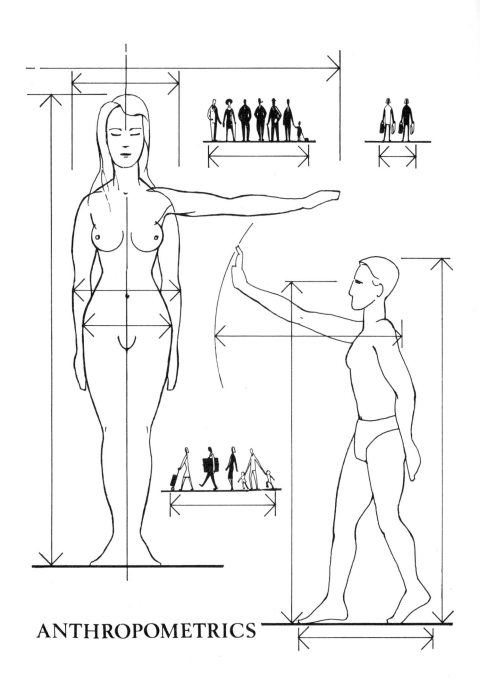

ANTHROPOMETRICS

collection and deliveries, where houses are served only by footways; there are many others.

The foregoing remarks refer to unaided human effort. When mechanical aids are taken into account, human capabilities are vastly extended. In regard to movement alone, the use of various kinds of horizontal and vertical transport has had, and still is having, profound effect on environmental design. Multi-storey blocks of offices and dwellings would not be feasible without lifts – the elevator made the skyscraper possible not construction techniques. And the development of ground transportation has probably been the greatest single factor in urban design, and the one about which so many planning problems still centre. In the nineteenth century the necessity for industrial workers to be within reasonable walking distance of their employment was the reason for the crowded housing conditions of that period. Later, the development of steam railways made it possible for office workers and others to move out of the towns and suburban sprawl began. Trams and buses similarly encouraged outer development, and then the private motor-car and uncontrolled population growth brought about the unsatisfactory conditions of the present day: choked roads, destroyed amenities, noise, fumes and other pollutions. Two solutions show hope: 'park and ride' or the barring of private vehicles from central areas requiring those who commute from a distance to park at the perimeter and proceed by public transport, for example, by electric railways or rapid transit buses; and the provision of court-yard housing back in the towns, but well laid out and designed with full regard to convenience, comfort and amenities, close to offices, shops, etc.

Planning elements

Before listing planning elements and their respective functional requirements, very briefly, the levels of planning – in the sense of the disposition of those elements – are national, regional and local.

Firstly, take Britain, excluding Northern Ireland, as an example of advanced organised planning, which is conveniently an island. The entire country is the responsibility of the central government acting through various Ministries for the framing and execution of a *national* policy with respect to the use and development of land, including agricultural land, new towns and town expansions, inland transport, generation and distribution of power, national parks and the countryside. At this level certain decisions have to be made directly in the national interest but much of the functions of central government departments are decentralised to *regional* organisations, of which England had eight, with Scotland and Wales (including Monmouthshire) each a separate region. In theory, and in fact, a region is an extensive area defined by a set of closely associated conditions, e.g. geographical, historic, administrative, etc., but in practice, and so far as the British regions are concerned, the basis is socio-economic. The objects of regional economic planning councils and boards are to help formulate plans having regard to the regions' resources, to advise on the implementation of the plans, and to advise on the regional implications of national economic policy. The collection and analysis of relevant information is an important part of the work. But, finally, actual physical planning is the responsibility of local authorities which are in England and Wales, councils of counties, county boroughs, the London authorities, and in some areas, joint planning boards.* Under the Town and Country Planning Act 1971, the county and county borough councils are required to prepare structure plans for the whole or, in certain circumstances, for parts of their area. The structure plan is a written statement, with diagrams and illustrations, which within the framework of national and regional policies *inter alia*, establishes aims, policies and general proposals and provides in turn a framework for local plans including action areas, and guidance for development control, which is another function of local authorities. It is at this local level that public participation is encouraged, and where the urban designers, developers, architects and surveyors become directly concerned. However, having sketched the administrative background, consideration can be given to the principal plan elements. These have been summarised as where people live, work, move and play. These categories are not distinct and separate, but realising this, the elements may nevertheless be grouped under those four headings as follows:

1. *Where people live.* Residential areas of all kinds including private and local authority housing estates and concomitant developments, e.g. private gardens, public open spaces, young children's play spaces, local shops, churches and chapels, community buildings, local services: fire, police, clinics, etc.
2. *Where people work.* Agriculture: farms, villages, market towns; fishing: villages, ports; industrial plants, trading estates; factories, mines; public utilities; offices, laboratories; defence establishments; central administrative and public buildings; central and regional shopping centres.
3. *Where people play.* National, regional and local parks, leisure areas; seaside and country resorts; sports grounds and stadia, playing-fields, racing plants; theatres, cinemas, entertainment centres, restaurants, cafes, pleasure gardens.

* The Local Government Bill 1971 in general places responsibility for preparing struc-ture plans on the new County Authorities and the preparation of local plans and the carrying out of development control on District Authorities.

living

Residential Areas including all kinds of dwellings and concomitant developments: private gardens, local open spaces and landscaping   Local Shops   Community Buildings   etc.

working

Agricultural and Forest Lands Farms and Market Towns Fishing Villages   Industrial Areas   Shopping, Commercial and Administrative Centres Defence Establishments   etc.

playing

National, Regional, and Local Parks and Leisure Areas Seaside and Country Resorts Playing Fields and other sports facilities Entertainment Centres   etc. etc.

moving
& COMMUNICATIONS

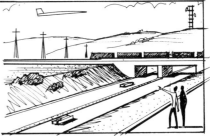

Roads, Railways, Waterways and associated buildings   Airports and Seaports   Viaducts, Bridges and Tunnels Transmission Cables and Pipe Lines   Telecommunications, etc

LAND USE GROUPINGS

4. *How people and goods move.* Roads, railways, waterways and associated buildings, airports, seaports; viaducts, bridges, tunnels; transmission cables and pipelines, etc.

It will be seen that such a listing is still in somewhat general terms, and is capable of being extended or rearranged, but let it suffice as a basis for the further consideration of some of the major planning elements.

7
Towns

There are many definitions of a town and many theories of town design. It is outside the scope of this book to go into these, although it may be remarked that new development should preferably be organic and evolutionary rather than 'ideal artifacts' conceived as complete and finite works.

It should be emphasised that whatever the town plan, it should give the greatest possible freedom to individuals by promoting and controlling developments in the interests of the community as a whole, and by providing for the physical and psychological needs outlined in the previous chapter. It should not be made to serve the interests of only a section of the community, commercial or otherwise, or of an authority.

In the design process, whether a renewal or an expansion of an existing town or a plan for a new town is concerned, from the very beginning visual considerations must enter into the discussions, deliberations and decisions. This must be so even at the formulation of a diagrammatic master layout stage, and notwithstanding its necessary flexibility and therefore the possibility – almost certainty – of subsequent changes. The importance of visual integrity has already been stressed and it is a reflection of efficient functional planning and of coherence; mention has also been made of some of the factors affecting urban form and composition.

Every town consists of:

(1) buildings and other structures;
(2) open and enclosed spaces (as defined later);
(3) circulations (vehicular and pedestrian);

arranged in various ways, but almost always in the following areas:

(*a*) Central core. Civic and administration buildings; main business and commercial premises; main shopping centre; main entertainments and cultural buildings; large and small enclosed spaces.

(*b*) Residential areas. Mainly dwellings and gardens, but also related local social and other community buildings, primary schools, local rest and play spaces, and perhaps smaller service and light industrial workshops; local shops.

(*c*) Industrial. Factories, workshops, warehouses (some may be in central area); utilities and plants.

(*d*) Recreation. Larger open spaces, parks, sports grounds, playing-fields, etc., which are linked with one another and the surrounding districts by footpaths and roads, and with the regional and national communications networks by roads and railways.

There are other elements, but the above are the main groupings and they will illustrate a number of points applicable generally.

Town centre

As the focus of town life is sometimes referred to as the heart of the city, the central area should have the greatest visual importance, be most highly organised in its relation of parts, its buildings and its spaces, with some degree of formality in its layout and dignity and refinement in its architecture.

It requires to have clear identity and, notwithstanding definition by physical features, e.g. bend of river, line of city walls, inner loop road, etc. the area should be defined also by the size, scale and unity of its buildings in contrast to the remainder of the town. The extent of these physical characteristics is proportionate to the size and importance of the town. This is not to say that there may not be higher or more extensive buildings elsewhere; there almost certainly will be. But in the centre should be found a concentration of big buildings of somewhat larger scale.

Open spaces, squares, piazzas and forecourts should be used to set off the more important buildings – as well as provide public assembly points (not traffic assembly!), so that they can be properly seen and appreciated, and also to provide landscaping opportunities.

The centre as a whole should be visible from various parts of the town and this consideration should take into account such things as the alignment viewpoints in the surrounding environs where this is topographically possible.

Town centre zones. There are a number of ways of grouping the constituent parts of a town centre. There cannot be a standard applicable to all towns, but the following zones, i.e. groups of buildings of similar use, are usually found:

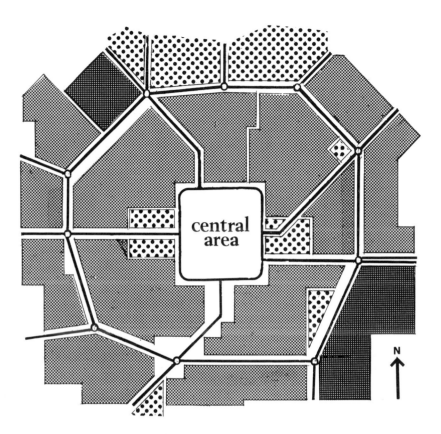

central

 residential

 industrial

 recreational

———— main roads

TOWN LAY·OUT
simplified diagram to show main areas

(*a*) principal administrative or civic group; social and cultural (public) buildings;

(*b*) main business and shopping, including ancillary service industries;

(*c*) major entertainment.

In some towns there are other zones such as university, polytechnic or cathedral.

In more detail, the building types that may be found or be appropriate in the centre are:

1. Local government office, e.g. town hall, council house; offices of statutory undertakings; central government offices, e.g. Labour and productivity, Defence recruiting, G.P.O. and Telephone exchange; central public library; museums.
2. Commercial and professional offices, particularly head or principal branch offices; banks and insurance offices; headquarters of institutions and societies.
3. Shops, department stores, market showrooms.
4. Restaurants, theatres, cinemas, entertainment centres.
5. Hotels, public-houses.
6. Principal religious (denominational) buildings: cathedrals, parish churches, etc.

Not necessarily all those listed above need be in the central area, but buildings which are undesirable, though not always harmful, because they militate against compactness and generate additional traffic, are:

1. Places of further education (unless existing).
2. Residential – *NOT* houses; perhaps flats, but better out of immediate centre.
3. Manufacturing and industrial – definitely not because of traffic problems in transport of materials, goods and workers (service only if ancillary to shops).
4. Warehouse – common but not to be encouraged.
5. Sports stadium.

Arrangement of zones. The arrangement of central zones will be influenced by local conditions: geographical, climatic, topographical, historical and relationships with surrounding areas. In some cases, the space allocation, while horizontal dispositions are most likely, may be in the nature of vertical zoning, i.e. on a multi-level basis. There is no set pattern but there are certain guiding ideas.

However, before dealing with individual zones, it should be mentioned that the central area as a whole should be central in fact as well as in name, i.e. it should be the geographical centre of the town, so far as this is possible, in a position of easy access from all other areas. It should be reasonably compact in order to reduce travel between various points, and therefore high density and tall building, with mechanical means of vertical communication, may be necessary, provided adequate open spaces and freedom of movement are not thereby jeopardised.

The civic group of administrative buildings, which, in the nature of things should be the most impressive architecturally, homogeneous in scale, character, materials and detail, should occupy the most prominent position, geographically as well as in the overall plan, in combination with a major open space, and use may well be made of landscaping and special features, e.g. monuments, fountains, etc.

Near-by buildings should reflect the scale and character of the civic group, but should not compete with it. There must be an order of importance.

Compatible groups are those of business and commerce, which require ready access to administration, but consideration should also be given to the inclusion within the area of restaurants and theatres so that interest is maintained at night. The civic zones should be away from industry, warehouses, railways or any source of undue noise and disturbance, such as heavy or considerable volume of traffic.

The commercial or business group, consisting mainly of offices must be served by public transport, which may well be underground or below ordinary street level. It need not be associated with the shopping area, although it is not unusual to find shops and showrooms on the ground floor of office buildings. However, in the new towns in Britain, the business area is usually set apart from the shopping centre.

In the case of a large town or a town that serves as a regional centre, the size of office accommodation may warrant a subdivision into two parts: (a) larger business and commercial firms, banks and insurance companies, and (b) professional, such as solicitors, architects, etc.

Visually, the buildings in the central area have to be considered: (a) at a distance; (b) at close range; (c) actually experienced by moving about them and in them. From afar, the siting and height of the buildings, whether grouped or possibly combined in multi-level complexes, should present a clear dominant in the overall urban composition when perceived in mass or silhouette. In this connection, the skylines as seen from various viewpoints and, in some cases, against a background, is of great importance. Confusion must be avoided, and the form must be cohesive, essentially simple and, although there are exceptions, without ragged, jagged and visually incomprehensible shapes jutting upwards in a disorderly array. The view from above should not be overlooked! From the air or from surrounding high ground, focal definition should be obvious by reason of the layout, size and disposition of buildings, open spaces and converging roads, although these need not necessarily be rigid radial patterns.

At closer range, when colour, texture, pattern and detail can be perceived as well as outline and form – indeed, outline and form may be of little significance – the principles referred to in previous chapters should receive full consideration.

In completely new developments there should be no difficulty in achieving not merely a visually satisfactory result but one of a high order of visual pleasure in all its parts. This assumes that the layout and buildings of the central areas are designed as a unified scheme, as of course they should be, and will be executed within a relatively short period of time.

However, in many cases, including some wholly or virtually new developments, construction cannot be carried out in this ideal way. Although there will be a master plan, and the imposing of various controls in regard to site coverage, heights of buildings and perhaps external materials, and although the main civic buildings and their immediate surroundings may be the work of one team of designers, buildings for commercial, entertainment, and other uses are likely to be individually designed and constructed over a number of years. Controls should always be minimum and progress in building design should not be held back. Restrictions must be such that they allow for inevitable changes in functional planning requirements and modes of construction. There must be freedom for innovations in design, but not for experiment, for which the proper place is in exhibitions. Nevertheless, the foregoing design principles should be observed. This may mean the vetting of designs by a competent advisory panel, acting in accordance with those principles, or preferably, by the good sense, appreciation of visual urban environmental requirements, and skill of the designers, who are strong-willed enough to resist the temptation, and perhaps the urgings of their clients, to perpetrate personal idiosyncrasies or to give way to the desire to be 'different'.

As regards redevelopment in an existing town, the same ultimate result should be the aim, but there are the all too obvious problems of inherited inadequate road layouts, insufficient open space, and the heterogeneous mixture of incongruous, chaotic buildings, many of which may be in poor condition. If such a situation is consistent over the area concerned, then wholesale clearance and rebuilding may be the best solution although this is not always easy to achieve. Often, however, there are some relatively new buildings worth retaining or buildings of historic value which it would be vandalism to destroy. If these can be incorporated into a new scheme, the remainder could be removed, either comprehensively or, as is more likely, in a piecemeal procedure followed by a replanning and rebuilding programme. What is important, however, is that the redevelopment is in keeping with the principles kept clearly in view from the beginning of the design process and throughout its implementation.

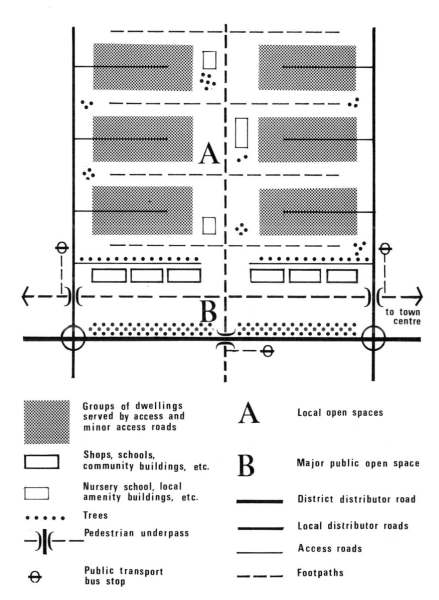

	Groups of dwellings served by access and minor access roads	**A**	Local open spaces
	Shops, schools, community buildings, etc.	**B**	Major public open space
	Nursery school, local amenity buildings, etc.		District distributor road
.....	Trees		Local distributor roads
—)|(— —	Pedestrian underpass		Access roads
⊖	Public transport bus stop	— — —	Footpaths

RESIDENTIAL AREA
diagram of basic lay·out

Residential areas

In older towns, residential accommodation was originally mixed in with other developments due to sporadic growth over hundreds of years from small settlements. Then, in the nineteenth century industrial expansion started in Britain with workers having to live close to places of employment. This condition continued but later public transport, e.g. trams, railways, buses and the private motor-car brought about perimeter or suburban housing estates. After the First World War, local authority housing and slum-clearance schemes and speculative private enterprise greatly extended the outward spread, chiefly in the form of houses, and also resulted in the construction of large and high blocks of flats in the near-central and inter- mediate parts of towns. This outer horizontal and inner vertical development in both old and new towns has continued on a greatly increased scale since the Second World War, and is a feature of urban areas in most countries.

The provision of residential accommodation is an involved and highly specialised subject, in which sociological, economic, technological and political factors have continually to be reassessed as changing habits and ideas of living, such as greater individual and family mobility, population stabilisation (and perhaps reduction) may make the standards and the solutions of today obsolete tomorrow. The following, however, are some of the design principles which might receive consideration in the context of the environment.

Siting of dwellings

The creation of convenient and pleasant environments for human physical and psychological needs remains a basic object. Firstly, therefore, dwellings should be where natural beauty exists or can be reasonably made by man (although good agricultural land is too precious in Britain and elsewhere to be so used) and where there is nothing ugly or offensive. Flat land is not essential; sloping or undulating sites provide opportunities for interesting layouts. Secondly, dwellings should be arranged in com- munities in conjunction with schools, shops, social facilities, open spaces and, possibly, acceptable employment. A nucleated system consisting of 'primary school catchment' districts, a number of which are linked to form a community about a centre (focal point), can become a defined residential area in the town plan. Physical definition may be given by the road net- work, e.g. main road connection from the town centre and other parts of the town leads to district distributors around the communities, within which local distributors serve the estates. Access and minor access roads provide vehicular approach to the dwellings. As well as roads, pedestrian networks

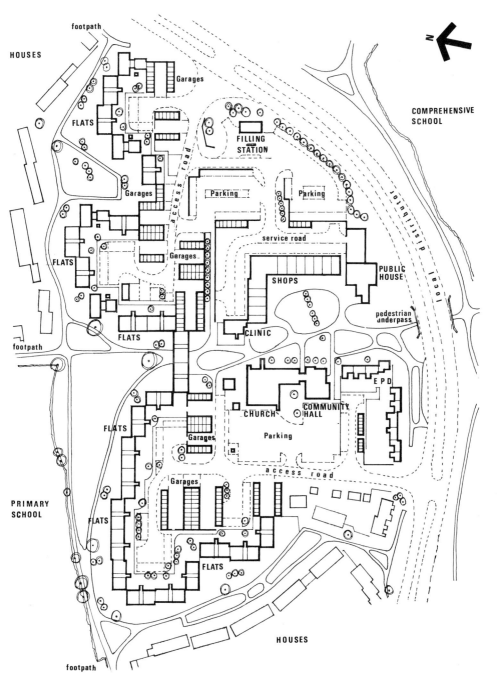

RESIDENTIAL AREA
example of district ~ neighbourhood ~ centre

71

are required for communication between dwellings and 'desire points', i.e. transport (bus stops), grouped garages, shops, schools, etc.; these should be short without undue deviation, but footpaths for leisure walking can meander to take in natural features.

Dwellings fall into two main categories: (1) houses, including bungalows; (2) flats or apartments, including maisonettes.

Houses

There are five types: (*a*) detached; (*b*) semi-detached; (*c*) terrace; (*d*) bungalow; (*e*) courtyard or patio. Design points are:

(*a*) Detached. If visually isolated, can be individually and distinctively designed, but if seen with others, mutual acknowledgement necessary in scale, colour, dominant texture, materials, etc.

(*b*) Semi-detached. Essentially a standard, economical design, therefore unaltered repetition and some formality of arrangement logical; monotony should be relieved by variations in building lines, use of curved roads, landscaping and interspersing with other *compatible* types of dwellings, not by imposed and thereby artificial individual idiosyncrasies of external treatment. Continuity can be given by use of link elements.

(*c*) Terraces. Considered better in appearance than semi-detached, while equally or more economic, because larger visual elements means less fragmentation of compositions, especially if there are common front spaces. Many possible variations in arrangements add interest, which is increased by informal landscaping.

(*d*) Bungalows. Similar considerations as detached houses. Grouping with avoidance of gross differences in materials, colours, detail, etc. necessary for visual acceptance.

(*e*) Courtyard (patio). Essentially conjoined dwellings of standard design in close, regular arrangement; high density offset by associated common open spaces. Various patterns, clusters and 'chain' arrangements (undulating ground) provide opportunities for interesting combined functional and visual compositions in which contrast of plain walls with fencing, play of light and shade, etc. are important elements. As with semi-detached, imposed external treatments unsatisfactory.

With all such residential developments, the appearance from above, from aircraft or high ground should receive consideration, particularly in regard to compact layouts. The extent of roofing, e.g. of a large number of single-storey courtyard houses, can present a visual problem.

View of grouped terrace houses showing common open space with footpath, grass and trees between low-fenced private gardens. This is part of the residential area, the centre of which is illustrated by the plan on page 71.

View of shops with maisonettes over (plan on page 71) showing traffic-free landscaped front open space. Service road, parking space and garages are at the rear.

Visual design of residential areas

The general principles of good design, which are common to all developments, apply but the following recommendations should be given consideration:

1. Arrangement of houses should be in defined clusters or groups both by layout and landscaping for visual compositions and social identification (neighbourliness), as well as for good aspect and prospect.
2. Use curving roads and informal layouts consistent with topography and other site conditions.
3. Use some mixture of different types of dwellings in each estate but in separate groups with due regard to overall visual effect; not heterogeneous.
4. Consistency of architectural character, i.e. scale, colour, texture, details, is essential in groups and generally throughout an estate. Same roof pitches.
5. Common front open spaces (see notes on streets) preferred, with private gardens at rear.
6. Integration of buildings, open spaces, roads and footways is necessary; avoid awkward shapes and 'left-over' pieces of land. Dwellings to be in discernible relationships to roads.
7. Landscaping to be free and 'natural' but controlled and botanically suitable, to give maximum relief and mutually advantageous contrast with buildings.
8. Placing of street names, light standards, post-boxes, litter-bins, seats, to be considered as elements of visual composition as well as what is required for use. Selection of lettering, shapes and colours to be in accordance with surroundings.
9. Houses on steeply sloping sites should generally run with contours. When on a hill rising from the town they should not crown the summit but stop short to permit the hill to act as 'backdrop'.

Flats

Flat (apartment) – single-storey dwelling over or under another; Maisonette (duplex) – two-storey dwelling over or under another; in blocks from as few as four units to several hundreds, ranging from low rental Local Authority rehousing schemes to luxury apartments.

Types of blocks: (1) three–four storeys without lifts; (2) high blocks with lifts. (*a*) long blocks with external balcony access or internal corridor; (*b*) tower blocks, usually four units per floor around central access and service core; (3) 'stepped' terraces. Flats are sometimes provided in combination with other developments in urban areas.

View of houses shown on plan below.

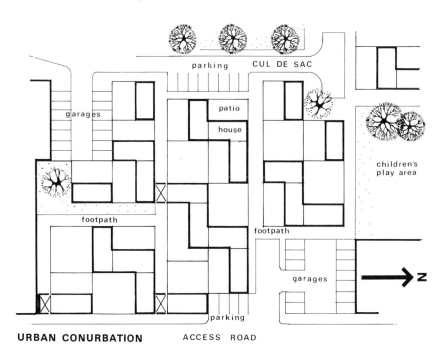

parking   CUL DE SAC

garages

patio

house

children's
play area

footpath

footpath

garages

N

footpath

parking

URBAN CONURBATION   ACCESS ROAD

Part plan of estate of two-storey patio houses in urban redevelopment scheme.

Flats and maisonettes meet the needs of increasing numbers of people. They are not ideal for young children, elderly infirm or garden enthusiasts, but for students, singles, childless couples or families with children over 10 years of age they are more convenient and easier to run than houses, and so allow greater personal freedom for creative and constructive activities.

The general advantages to society are: more economical use of land, saving of good agricultural land, more compact towns with consequent savings on transport, e.g. roads, vehicles, oil, etc., in individuals' time; also in provision of services.

Visual considerations of flats. Flats are essentially repeated identical units and for all but small blocks corresponding construction systems are appropriate; plan and structure patterns should be frankly expressed (see previous notes on pattern). While regard must be paid to near-by buildings, blocks are usually sufficiently isolated for this not to be unduly restrictive. Basic patterns of façades result from a unit plan and structure, usually rectilinear in shape and form, in which separate private or common access balconies can relieve 'flatness' by introducing possibilities of strong shadows into the compositions. Scale will be set by domestic dimensions of units. Colours, textures, materials and details can be controlled in accordance with the principles already given.

Siting of flats. Apart from street blocks, which are subject to design conditions so applicable, sites must be adequate to allow placing to the best advantages for aspect, prospect and adequate daylighting; this will usually automatically ensure convenient access, privacy, insulation from external noise and fire risks, and at the same time permit full visual perception of each block alone and in combination other blocks and other buildings and against its background for proper environmental appreciation.

Landscaping

The layout and planting of free areas of sites are important for physical and visual amenity value; paved walks and play spaces, seats, informal disposition of trees and plants – but not 'itty-bitty' gardens – are contributory elements to overall design.

Roads

As arrangement and spacing of blocks is the first consideration, the access road layout must conform, perhaps as a 'loop' from the local distributor linking a number of blocks, and so providing not only vehicular and pedestrian access but also service access and parking for visitors. All these are elements of the visual composition and must be considered as such as well as the functional purposes from which they are derived. Similarly with parking for residents which, according to circumstances, may be (1) on

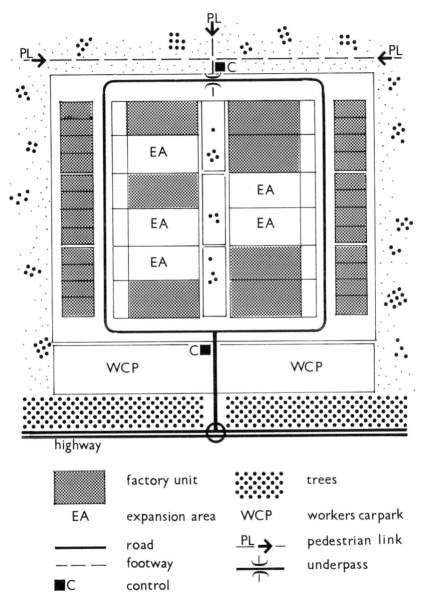

![factory unit]	factory unit	![trees]	trees
EA	expansion area	WCP	workers carpark
road	PL →_	pedestrian link
footway	⊥	underpass
■C	control

INDUSTRIAL AREA (ESTATE)
diagram of basic lay·out

ground floor of small blocks; (2) in grouped surface garages; (3) below general ground level or in a basement with direct access to lifts.

Industrial developments

There are three principal categories for design considerations. They are:

1.. Major installations. Siting is determined by essential functional needs, e.g. convenient access to raw materials, water supply, distribution system, etc. and to satisfactory means of disposal of wastes. Relatively few workers are employed, and site is preferably located away from towns. Examples are: power stations, oil refineries, etc.
2. Large manufacturing plants. These employ a high ratio of workers, and must be readily accessible from existing or new residential areas, and often located around perimeters of towns. Examples are: aircraft and motor-car factories, textile mills, food-processing and packing plants, etc.
3. Light industries. Small factories producing small articles are best grouped in industrial (trading) estates, convenient to national road network and with easy access for workers. Usually located on the perimeter or within towns, sometimes close to residential areas if there is no nuisance.

1. Major installations present special problems by reason of size, location and associated activities, e.g. extraction of raw materials, treatment of effluents, but visual satisfaction can be combined with functional efficiency – the two aspects should be inseparable – and while each case requires individual design, the following are general considerations that should be taken into account:

(a) Within the limits of practical and economic constraints, alternative locations and layouts should be studied to find the best disposition of the main elements in relation to existing land forms and backgrounds, and to achieve good compositional effects from varying viewpoints.
(b) Subordinate elements should be grouped in orderly arrangements; sites tidied, and waste and rubbish cleared as they accumulate. For integration and visual cohesion, common design characteristics, including colours, signs, lettering, etc. should be used and maintained throughout.
(c) Landscaping should be used as part of the design, e.g. (i) massed trees and shrubs to give firm base-line, and to provide contrast in direction to vertical towers, chimneys, masts, etc.; (ii) grassing of non-operational land for grazing (cheaper than mowing); (iii) modelling of land forms to assist relating of structures to the ground;

Views of the Estate

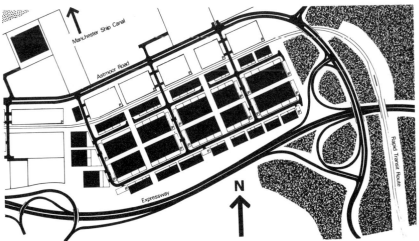

Runcorn New Town
Astmoor Industrial Estate

(iv) amenity planting : flowering trees are better than flowers as they are more in scale, but if flowers are used they should be massed or grouped in containers near administration buildings and entrances where they can be appreciated at close range.

(*d*) Colours should be studied in regard to distant and near views : from afar, constructional or cladding self-coloured materials dominate, e.g. concrete, asbestos cement, glass, etc. and are visually satisfactory together with large painted areas if they are neutral such as : silvery aluminium, warm greys and light browns, all generally in harmony so that masses are clearly perceived and there is no violent conflict with natural surroundings ; for close views, relatively minor elements may be in bright industrial colours – also for safety identification – blue, red, yellow, orange, etc., with any supporting framework in one other colour throughout. Black should be used where soiling is inevitable. In certain cases, interesting effects result from forms and colours of the plant seen through glazed façades.

Power stations

Power stations, which are among the largest industrial installations, can be classified according to source of energy :

1. Hydro-electric. Sited at waterfalls, dams, etc. and therefore usually in country away from habitations. They are in scale with surroundings. Foregoing design considerations apply.
2. Thermal
(*a*) Coal. Require railway or waterway to bring fuel, and considerable water supply for cooling ; therefore located close to a river, lake, etc. They were formerly sited in large towns to be close to main consumers and so minimise transmission costs, but size and scale conflicts with those of normal buildings, and dust, smoke and steam are undesirable urban pollutants ; with dispersal of industries and modern transmission networks, they are now regarded as regional elements to be sited accordingly.
(*b*) Oil/Gas. Less nuisance than coal, but similar considerations. Oil-fired stations are most economic if near refineries.
(*c*) Nuclear reactors. As with all power stations water supply and good soil-bearing capacity to support the heavy structures are main practical requirement. Often located on estuaries.

Power transmission lines

Transmission of electrical power is mainly by overhead cables, which are increasing in number and heights to meet the growing domestic and industrial demands. They are regarded as a serious visual threat to the land-

Estuary-located
nuclear power
station at Bradwell-
on-Sea (above);
the view shows the
massed, unified
range of efficient
buildings in green-
field setting.

Part of
Hydrocarbon
Reforming Plant at
Avonmouth (right).
Although exposed
plant of this kind is
complicated, the
functional, orderly
arrangement of the
forms, shapes, lines
and colours provide
considerable visual
interest and
satisfaction.

LARGE INDUSTRIAL PLANTS

Examples

ELECTRICITY PYLONS AND CABLES

400 kV suspension towers and transmission lines. The view shows the cultivation of crops under and around the towers, which are examples of framed structures.

scape, but as the cost of underground cables is so much greater than overhead wires, the situation has to be accepted until new systems of generating, storing and transmitting power are developed. However, the siting of new transmission lines should be carefully considered with due regard to amenity from the outset. Areas of outstanding natural beauty should be protected, even at the increased cost of underground installations or diversions, and the running of lines along skylines should be avoided. Elsewhere, for the present, it must be a matter of objective judgement. Pylons and cables are not inherently ugly. They can add interest by providing contrast in flat, featureless landscapes, and in average areas they can be assimilated by proper integration into existing surroundings and developments.

2. Large industrial units and factory complexes covering extensive areas and employing large numbers of workers are mainly single-storey buildings. These structures require flat sites with convenient links to national road networks and perhaps to railways and docks. They are best located on the edges of towns where they can be surrounded by open land, with clear definition in relation to other units; this permits independent architectural composition as well as providing room for expansion. Residential areas should not be close, but there must be good communication, rapid transit, between workers' homes and places of employment. Where the units have to be located near raw materials or sources of power far from existing towns, new residential and associated developments will have to be established along with connecting roads.

Visual design considerations are as before. The buildings are usually low and somewhat uninteresting in form, although there may be vertical contrast provided by chimneys, water towers, silos. Grouped tall trees are likely to be an advantage. Recent tendencies to depart from the conventional compact 'square' production line layouts and adopt linear layouts gives greater opportunities for interesting planting and general landscaping.

3. Industrial or trading estates for light industries are in one ownership, either private or local authority. Roads and services are provided and, in some cases – which is much to be preferred from the visual design aspect – standard unit factory buildings, usually single-storey. Sites are necessarily level, and are laid out with regular and rectangular plots and roads, but if the buildings are well-designed or at least compatible, the estates can reach, with the careful placing of uniform street furniture, lettering, etc. a high standard of functional and visual efficiency and pleasantness of working conditions. A surrounding screen of trees with additional internal landscaping can help to achieve this end.

8
Roads and Bridges

Roads

Roads have been described as paved strips of land surfaces primarily for the use of vehicles, which at the present time, means motor vehicles. There are two main categories or roads: (1) highways — the principal traffic routes connecting towns, villages and industrial areas, with limited access to properties, and (2) access roads — connecting highways to sites and buildings. Together, these two categories comprise a communications network making it possible to travel thereon from any point to any other point.

In Britain, roads are classified as: (*a*) motorways, from which no direct access to properties and no pedestrians and bicycles are permitted; (*b*) class A, the main national roads; (*c*) class B, less important national roads; (*d*) class C, less important than class B, but more important than local roads; (*e*) unclassified (!), local roads and country lanes.

For planning purposes, highways are usually referred to as National, Regional, Primary Distributors, District Distributors and Local Distributors — the last three as urban roads — in a descending order of functional use and permitted speeds. As well as this distributor hierarchy are the access and minor roads.

It is the district and, to some extent, local distributors that should define land use areas and zones, sometimes referred to as environmental areas, and tie together or integrate them into the overall plan. Neither they nor any highway should divide or break up an area, as happens when a main traffic route passes through a village.

Siting of highways

The positions of many of the older roads were determined by historic reasons, which are no longer valid, so that the routes are not the best for present-day and projected traffic requirements, and therefore many improvements such as straightening, widening and levelling have to be carried out, or they have to be superseded by new roads. The location of such new roads requires consideration of practical and engineering aspects, e.g. topography, natural features, subsoils, existing developments; of economic factors, e.g. costs of acquiring land and buildings; as well as construction costs. A straight line road is not always the cheapest or most useful, and taking land use and environmental considerations into account, and also social, e.g. safety, noise and visual considerations, a more realistic cost/efficiency criterion can be established.

Visual considerations of roads

1. Long, straight stretches of road are monotonous and tiring to the eye, although difficult to argue against in level featureless landscapes, where other means must be introduced to afford visual relief. However, in most cases, deviations in the routes are possible within engineering and economic limits, and the danger of driver fatigue lessened.

2. Highways should not slash across the countryside or cause scars, except during construction, even if Nature does heal – in some countries quicker than in others –, but steps must be taken to blend and integrate highways into the rural scene. Not that new roads should be regarded as alien intrusions, but as additional man-made features in what is already a man-made environment, into which they should be skilfully woven or fitted.

3. Existing natural beauty should be preserved and made use of in maintaining interest to road-users, and for compositional elements of the modified landscape. Existing trees and hedges should be incorporated in the design wherever possible.

4. High banks and close fencing or any other view-preventing obstacles, except perhaps for unavoidable short stretches to screen ugly developments or provide wind-breaks, give an undesirable hemmed-in feeling.

5. Routes should be along lines of demarkation or of boundaries of different land uses, e.g. between forest and farmland, orchards and hill pasture, urban developments and green belts, or along the bank of a river; this provides satisfying visual planning definition.

6. Where there are dual-carriageways, they need not be parallel but, where the topography permits, central reservations can be varied in width and the carriageways can be at different levels. It may be more economic to have such arrangements, as well as helping to prevent glare from opposing headlights. The planting of shrubs along central reservations also has the latter effect in addition to amenity value.

7. Cuttings and embankments should be rounded at top and bottom, and be softened in form by grass and plants, which are also means of stabilising loose soil. They may be made flatter than the strict engineering maximum angle of repose.

8. While uniform planting of trees, e.g. an avenue, may be appropriate in certain urban areas, it is unsuitable for roads in the country, not only because of monotony, but also because of the irritating and potentially dangerous effect on the eyes of sunlight through such regular planting. Trees should be informally disposed in groups composed of indigenous types forming links with the existing landscape. Small flowering trees which may be suitable for residential streets appear incongruous along major highways.

9. Boundary walls or fences should not be parallel to roads for long stretches; some deviations provides interest. Boundaries should preferably be of local types, e.g. stone walling, hedges, etc. When retaining walls have to be used, although walls are usually more expensive than banking of earth, stone and brick of local varieties might be used for low walls, but reinforced concrete is more likely to be necessary for high walls. Visually, the finish or facing is the important consideration and, in this connection, the effects of weathering have to be taken into account. The frank expression of concrete, albeit suitably treated, e.g. exposed aggregate, grooved, as described for bridges, is generally better than a veneer of another material, especially imitation masonry concrete blocks. Contrived decorative patterns are also better avoided, but horizontal or vertical emphasis according to shape or desired 'direction', which can be effected by recessing in the arrangement of formwork, if boldly done, is visually acceptable.

Much of the foregoing is a matter of landscaping, natural and designed. In regard to urban roads, it might be mentioned here that the provision of trees and associated planted areas adds greatly, not only to residential but to all developments. They help to meet an almost universal human desire for natural beauty in daily life. There is, too, the value of perceived seasonal changes, even in the tropics, that trees afford. For long-term residents, the view looking out from a dwelling is more important than its own appearance, and this continual change of growing things adds interest to the view, apart from the beauty on any one day. At all times, trees and plants provide by their structure, colour and movement, contrast to the forms, colours and static-ness of the buildings and roads in the urban environment.

Roundabouts

As well as acting as traffic route foci in a practical way, roundabouts are also centres of visual interest both for travellers and observers. Mounding

Slender and
unobtrusive steel
lighting columns
along spine of
motorway to
Heathrow — London
Airport. Attractive by
day (below) and
efficient by night (left).

and planting can be used to reduce or obviate headlight glare; this can be achieved by low-level evergreen bushes, but some informally arranged tall trees increases the effectiveness of visual significance. In rural areas, the modelling and planting should accord with the surrounding landscape. Any signs should be kept to a minimum and be kept low. Lighting standards are better placed elsewhere. Cottage garden flowers regularly spaced, tiny rustic stone walls, and other 'twee' features should not be permitted. Roundabouts are no place for flowers, although flowering shrubs may be acceptable.

Interchanges

Finishes of structures should be as previously described for retaining walls, and grassing and planting generally of associated grounds should be as for roadsides, trees being arranged informally.

Railings

Railings in connection with roads are best of standard types with close vertical bars to prevent small children crawling through. This design is visually satisfactory, and preferable to tubular types which, with mesh panels for safety, are unattractive. However, to motorway bridges and flyovers where there are no footways, horizontal rails are permissible and are visually more in accord with high-speed traffic.

Signs, advertisements

As referred to elsewhere, in many countries directional and informative road signs are largely standardised in design and types of lettering and symbols for speedy recognition. These are generally visually acceptable, but in urban areas many signs are bewildering and difficult to follow because they are badly placed or confusing.

Advertisements are strictly controlled in Britain, but occasional sale notices are sometimes allowed to remain too long until they become torn, dirty and altogether unsightly, and homemade wayside vendors signs are often visually objectionable.

Road surfaces

There are many road finishes, e.g. macadam, asphalt, concrete, wood block, rubber, etc. in common use. Practical considerations, e.g. safety and durability, are paramount, but visually, any even colour and texture is satisfactory, provided the surface is glare free. But variations in colour or abrupt changes of materials not related to changes of use or surroundings can be momentarily distracting and perhaps dangerous as they might cause drivers to take wrong turnings; conversely, the use of different materials or colours for different classes of roads or between roads and verges can reinforce directional signs.

Bridges

Bridges and similar structures, e.g. viaducts, interchanges, are of particular interest and value in the study of visual design. Essentially for practical use, i.e. to make it possible for vehicles and/or pedestrians to pass over physical obstacles, the expression of this function and of its construction can hardly be disguised, yet such artefacts are by common agreement among the most visually satisfying in the built environment.

Types of bridges

1. Simply supported *beams* and slabs are the earliest types historically, e.g. tree-trunks across a stream. They can now be of timber, metal – usually steel – or reinforced concrete for short spans, or in the form of steel lattice or box girders, or pre-stressed concrete beams for longer spans.
2. *Arches* are used for single or multiple spans:
   (*a*) in masonry, i.e. stone or brick, generally for short spans, of which there are many historical examples. Firm foundations and strong abutments are required. The characteristic form results from the structure, and colour and texture from the chosen material and its treatment;
   (*b*) in reinforced concrete, the arch usually supports a horizontal roadway with open spandrels. Longer spans than with masonry are possible, and such bridges are lighter in appearance;
   (*c*) in steel arch forms, the roadway or railway can be hung as a chord connected to a single arch by inclined members, which is known as the 'bowstring' type, or, for long spans, by suspension from a lattice arch as the Sydney Harbour Bridge. In both kinds the arch form dominates the design and the geometrical arrangement of contrasted curved and straight members provides satisfactory visual interest. Note: the arrangement known as the 'vierendeel' truss, which is similar in appearance to the 'bowstring' type but with intermediate vertical members and rigid joints is not an arch in the structural sense but a type of beam.
3. *Suspension* bridges are used for very long spans; they are the only feasible type for over 600 metres. An exciting design, often enhanced in appearance by location over a wide river or an arm of the sea. The

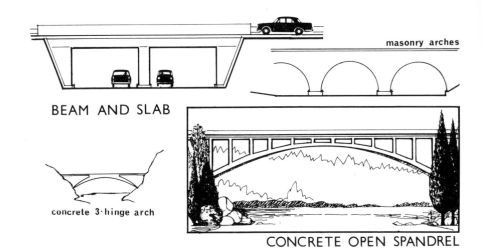

masonry arches

BEAM AND SLAB

concrete 3·hinge arch

CONCRETE OPEN SPANDREL

STEEL ARCH

steel–box stayed-girder structure

perspective

diagrammatic elevations

SUSPENSION

BRIDGES

EXAMPLES

Elegant reinforced concrete footbridge over road in residential area providing safe access to local shopping centre.

PEDESTRIAN BRIDGES

Footpath and reinforced concrete bridge over motorway enclosed by means of standard steel and glass units for maximum weather protection in exposed position.

contrast between the straight verticality of the towers, the lightness and curvature of the main cables and filament-like hangers, and the slightly cambered lattice girder roadway is dynamic and dramatic. Sheer size dominates the landscape in all directions for considerable distances. Minor elements require to be of utmost simplicity, any ornament or ostentation anywhere being ridiculous and irrelevant.

4. *Cable-stayed girder* bridges also make use of cables to support a continuous box section. Appearance is visually satisfying, but they lack the grace of the suspension type.

5. *Movable* bridges, e.g. swing, bascule, vertical lift transporter, pose special problems but, while each must be judged individually, they can generally be visually appreciated as large-scale machinery if correctly designed with honest expression of function and structure. Dirt and cluttered surroundings often adversely affect their appearance, but in properly maintained environments and by the use of colours selected with due regard to functional parts, climate and background, they can be more than merely visually acceptable. Often it is the silhouette, seen against the sky, that counts most, as it does in the case of pithead winding gear and similar industrial constructions.

6. *Footbridges* over busy roads: as the load is relatively light and spans comparatively short, they should be slender in design. It is best if the bridge and its approaches, i.e. steps and, possibly, ramps, are combined in one structure. As most bridges of this type are beams, full use should be made of cambering to gain height and reduce the number of approach steps. Parapets should not be solid: simple railings with closely-spaced verticals are best and they maintain the desired lightness of effect.

7. *Railway* bridges, because of long, heavy moving loads must be strong and this means deep steel beams for relatively short spans with corresponding massive masonry or concrete piers and abutments, and heavy steel girder arch forms for longer spans.

Visual design considerations of bridges

With all bridges and like structures their relationships to their settings is important. Small bridges of masonry arch construction may be influenced by the architectural character of any near-by buildings, but large bridges and those of long spans must inevitably be in definite contrast. The bigger or longer a bridge the less choice of design, which will be dictated by practical and economic considerations. But all bridges should be simple, i.e. straightforward in expression of function and structural principle. Especially with larger bridges, the clean lines of basic form should be free

Vertical lift bridge over the Canal de Willebroek, the Brussels Ship Canal.

MOVABLE BRIDGES

Correctly designed with unadorned expression of function/structure, such bridges can be appreciated as large-scale machinery. It is often the dirty and cluttered surroundings that adversely affect appearance, as in this example. But in properly laid out environments, with the use of colour, selected having due regard to functional parts, climate and background, they can be more than visually acceptable. Often it is the silhouette seen against the sky that counts most.

from non-functional additions, which add weight and therefore increase cost.

Each bridge should have some individuality, but this should not be blatantly contrived but should be evolved from an appropriate design, which together with the landscape will create a distinctive composition. Similarly, proportions should not be imposed, but should arise from construction. To the unprejudiced eye they will then look right; if imposed they will look wrong.

Scale is a matter of relation to surroundings. A small town bridge should be in scale with adjacent buildings in the urbanity of its treatment and refinement of detail in regard to its approaches, parapets or balustrades, lighting standards, abutments, etc. But a bridge remote from habitations, perhaps carrying a railway and so seen normally from a distance, can be bolder in scale. It can be in scale with the landscape, as it were, and not with humans.

Bridges of many spans preferably should have equal spans but if some have to be greater than others, there should be some discernible order in the arrangement. Depths of beams should be proportionate to spans throughout, or if arches are used, the ratio of rise to span should be consistent. A single centre support might give rise to 'duality', but this is less of a visual detraction than might be thought; beam bridges over dual carriageways, for example, can have supports rising from the central reservation if the beam, as it should structurally, appears to carry through.

Approaches to bridges often involve complex junctions of roads and slip roads, and here landscaping as described for highways generally applies.

Materials, finishes and colours of bridges

The study of bridge design with particular reference to materials, finishes and colours has relevance to many other structures, to which the following recommendation can also be applied:

Masonry, that is, brick and stone, are little used at the present time for major bridges, although these materials may be justified for small spans where the character of the surroundings strongly indicates the use of one or the other. Stone bridges might fittingly be finished with a rough texture in country districts, whereas a smooth or ashlar finish might be more appropriate in urban situations.

Steel bridges, apart from simple beam types – and they should not be exceptions so far as the principle is concerned – are almost impossible to 'disguise' by applied facings. The forms, patterns and rhythms are determined by the nature of the material and the modes of its construction. The only free choice affecting appearance is the colour of the painting, which is necessary for protection of the metal. In this connection, the use

Applied finishes, such as sand and cement roughcast (right), granular minerals bonded in vinyl-based resins, mosaics, tiling, etc. more suitable for relatively small areas, or areas divided into panels, because of variations in application and, in some cases, effects of thermal movement. Design measures to prevent staining essential.

SURFACE FINISHES EXAMPLES

see also illustrations on pages 24, 28 and 29

On major concrete surfaces of civil engineering works, such as bridge abutments, elevated roadways, etc., exposed aggregates or heavy rough vertical grooving (right) or similar formwork produced finishes more satisfactory in imparting character and in minimising effects of staining and irregular weathering. Note comparatively smooth recessed border to example illustrated.

of a uniform colour throughout is generally regarded as being best, although the principal functional parts may be distinguished by different colours, but preferably not more than three such colours. Main colours should tend towards neutral, while having a discernible bias towards a definite hue, for example : blue-grey or red-grey (brown) are suitable for urban bridges. However, the colours of the surroundings or background must be taken into account, and the effects of reflections on to and from river or sea of shadows on land or water, and of silhouettes should be considered.

Incidentally, strong or vivid greens are certainly to be avoided in country areas, where they will conflict with the natural hues. It is suggested that parapets and railings should be lighter in colour than the rest in order to emphasise their lightness in weight and non-structural nature.

The use of *concrete* for bridges results in design characteristics of homogeneity and slenderness, which should be further expressed by sharpness or crispness of detail, clean lines, and smoothness of finish; this does not preclude the use of exposed aggregate or hammered finishes provided there are smooth margins and sharp arrises to such areas.

On the broader surfaces of piers and abutments, including those to steel bridges, a deliberately rough texture may well be given to express strength and to minimise the effect of staining and irregular weathering. This applies also to viaducts, elevated roadways, large retaining walls, and anywhere where there are large areas of unbroken concrete faces. Examples of treatment are :

1. leaving of boardmarks from timber formwork in the casting of the concrete ;
2. use of formwork linings of various kinds also to produce the required texture in the casting ;
3. exposing of the aggregate by: (*a*) surface retarder followed by wire brushing ; (*b*) grit blasting ; (*c*) chipping or hammering. These methods make it possible to introduce colour by pre-selection of suitably coloured coarse aggregates.

Veneers of other materials can be applied, but this is only justified where there is the possibility of actual physical contact by the public. Whatever the nature of the veneer, it must be expressed as such and not made to appear structural, for example, slabs of stone or tiles should have both horizontal and vertical joints carrying through in straight lines – staggered bonding implies structure. Tiles and mosaic are both risky facings because of thermal movements.

9
Spaces and Streets

Planning and urban design are as much concerned with spaces as with buildings and other structures. Spaces are not just the areas left over; they have to be designed as part of the environmental organisation, wherein there must be complete, lucid and readily appreciated relationships.

Open spaces

It is the 'natural landscape', e.g. fields, moors, hills and valleys, stretches of water, the broad open space which provides the background and setting for man-made structures and connecting links of roads, railways and services. This background has always to be considered in regard to mutual effects on and of developments, both practically and visually, including views from the air.

Then there is the extension of natural open spaces, the spaces consisting mainly of grass, trees, plants and flowers, into built-up areas, as parks, recreation grounds, public and private gardens. These intra open spaces, together with *large* town squares which may be described as urban open spaces, have carefully to be designed taking into account:

function and use;
spatial composition – widths and lengths of spaces and heights of surrounding buildings;
connections and sequences;
human factors of scale and atmosphere;
detail features and planting;

so that spaces, buildings and structures are all integrated into a unified design.

Enclosed spaces

These are urban spaces, usually wholly or almost wholly paved, which are small enough to have a sense of enclosure. They have a more intimate relationship with the buildings immediately surrounding them. Examples are: forecourts, internal courts, precincts, residential enclaves. The foregoing considerations in respect of urban open spaces apply plus considerations of light, air, microclimate and acoustics. Generally, there is some emphasis on protection and shelter.

Urban spaces may be symmetrical in plan shape for reasons of formality, in conjunction with a symmetrical arrangement of buildings, or irregular in shape with a varied arrangement of buildings. Planting and detail should correspond with whichever shape is used.

It should be remembered that as with urban spaces they are seen from buildings and that buildings are seen from them.

Urban spaces can be so arranged that it is possible for pedestrians to traverse the town in different directions, away from the noise and disturbance of most streets, by a sequence of interconnected spaces and links that may pass under or through buildings. Variations of use, shape, sizes and perhaps levels, and the inclusion of planting and special features, can provide great interest and visual pleasure.

Changes of levels in urban spaces, where justified by the nature of sites or functional requirements, provide excellent opportunities for exploiting means of additional visual interest: steps, railings, balustrades, pools, fountains, paving patterns, because of the increased range of viewpoints which are higher or lower than normal.

Spaces at focal-points in town layouts may, according to size, be classified either as open or enclosed. They are variously described as: agora, forum (historical), place, square, plaza, centre, etc. As functional nodes, as well as elements of reference and orientation in the street plan, they can be used as places of assembly, resort, rest and general amenity. In most towns at the present time, the larger urban spaces have become areas of public and private traffic circulation and often extensive car parking, thus creating audible and visual disturbance. In new developments, urban spaces should be kept free from vehicles, other than for essential services, unless specifically intended for traffic.

It is best in all cases if there are only one or two conspicuous entrances to an urban space so that the sense of enclosure is not dissipated. The skylines of buildings around spaces are particularly important, as they are seen more prominently than from a street; confusion and excessive irregularity should be avoided. The central parts of spaces should not be cluttered with independent features; these are better arranged towards the sides, although one major monument, or two or three in very large areas, may well be so sited.

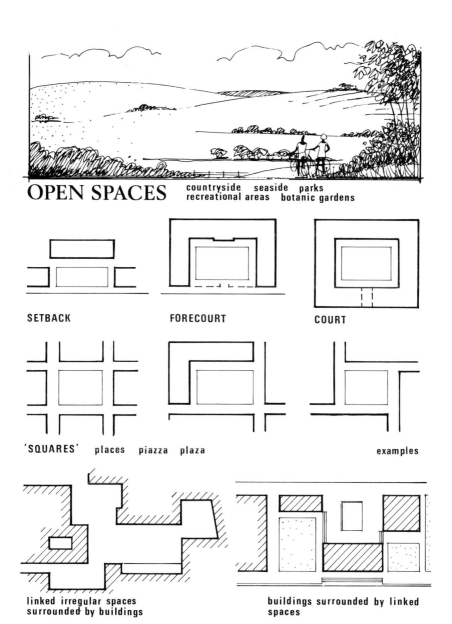

OPEN SPACES
countryside   seaside   parks
recreational areas   botanic gardens

SETBACK

FORECOURT

COURT

'SQUARES'   places   piazza   plaza   examples

linked irregular spaces
surrounded by buildings

buildings surrounded by linked
spaces

ENCLOSED SPACES

Street design

A single building or any structure standing by itself is perceived by colour, texture, light and shade, and perhaps by pattern, form, shape, line and detail. It can be seen from varying viewpoints in relation to its surroundings and possibly against a landscape or other background. The three-dimensional aspect of its visual appreciation is of paramount importance. This applies also to a group of buildings but in much of urban design buildings adjoin one another or are closely adjacent, so that visual emphasis is more on the two-dimensional design of façades and on horizontal continuity; in other words, on street architecture.

In the sense the word is used here, a street is a more or less continuous line of buildings along a roadway; the buildings are not necessarily of the same design. A terrace is a line of continuous unit buildings, usually houses, designed as a whole. A terrace can almost always be perceived as a single composition, but a street, unless short, is often a series of compositions seen in changing perspective as the spectator moves along it.

A street does not need to consist of near-uniform units throughout its length, or even for long stretches, provided there is a general unity of colour, texture, proportions and scale. Indeed, a long street of identical units – an extended terrace, as it were – can become dull and monotonous, particularly if straight, no matter how interesting the design of the individual unit may be. This is because, after the initial impact of the first seeing has been digested repetition produces a lessening response. So while some lengths of standardisation are acceptable, e.g. terraces, elements of ordered variety and of emphasis and punctuation should be introduced into street design. There must be what has been termed 'good manners' between neighbouring buildings, but reasonable freedom of expression is permissible. What has to be avoided is the degeneration of street architecture into a jumble of unrelated façades.

Skylines may be varied within the limits of balanced composition, but continual changes of horizontal levels are restless and visually unsatisfactory. 'Natural breaks' at road junctions are opportunities for differences in form and detail design of the corner buildings. Some sections of the street may have buildings set back from the general frontages, not arbitrarily, but for some valid reason like the provision of a forecourt to a more important building, at which point tree planting and other amenity features may be appropriate. In other cases, planned gaps may be provided in order to obtain views of the countryside, of mountains, lakes or the sea. But purposeless gaps (gashes) are an interruption to the sense of continuity and should be avoided. As well as the setting back of whole buildings or lengths of façades, the ground storey only may be omitted for connections with courts or other thoroughfares.

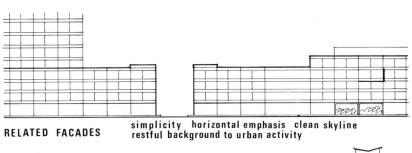

RELATED FACADES
simplicity horizontal emphasis clean skyline
restful background to urban activity

UNRELATED FACADES
irregular verticality cluttered skyline
confusing and disturbing background

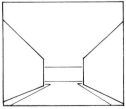 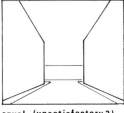 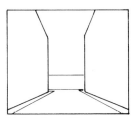

wider than high   equal (unsatisfactory?)   higher than wide

RELATIVE PROPORTIONS – SPACE BETWEEN BUILDINGS

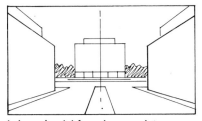 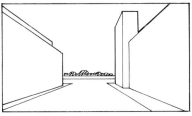

balanced axial formal approach to
symmetrical dominant terminal

end feature·one side in the
absence of strong terminal

STREET DESIGN

101

When buildings occur on both sides of a street, it is not necessary for them in any particular section to be the same height and appearance, except where extreme formality has to be achieved, e.g. an avenue about an axis of symmetry leading to a strong terminal feature with which it is related, but there should always be the same harmonious relationship between the two sides that should exist between neighbouring buildings on either side.

Mention of the two sides of the street brings to mind consideration of the distance between them. A street is, in a sense, a long, sometimes a very long, and comparatively narrow enclosed space. It is generally held that the width of the space and the height of the buildings should be such that one is appreciably greater than the other for satisfactory visual effect. When the height is the greater, there is more sense of enclosure and coherence, although, less desirably, confinement; conversely, when the width is the greater, there is an open and spacious effect, but some loss of unity and, in the absence of life and movement of cars and people, perhaps a feeling of bleakness and depression – the 'prairie' effect.

It is an accepted principle that a street is visually most satisfactory when the carriageway and footways, the horizontal planes, are closely integrated with the vertical façades of the buildings, that is, when there is no obstructing element, such as a wall, high railing, hedge or an elaborate garden. If the façades do not rise straight from the pavement or footway, a level stretch of paving or lawn is preferred, the latter giving an opportunity for tree planting. In the town itself, this fusion of roads, footways and buildings is readily achieved but in residential areas, the idea of unfenced open space on the roadside of terrace dwellings has come into comparatively recent use in Britain. It is by no means accepted by everyone, although common practice in North America and elsewhere.

Where grassed or landscaped areas are provided in front of street buildings it is important that the paved links, i.e. footpaths, between pavements and buildings are of the same material and pattern. Paving patterns generally should be related to building design, and should not just happen.

Tree planting along streets is a big subject, and further reference will be made later. The value of such planting is not only for its own intrinsic interest of tree structure, foliage and blossoms, but also as a means of providing visual contrast in form, colour and texture to buildings and other man-designed works.

Sometimes, to preserve street continuity, horizontal linking elements such as minor buildings, screen walls and fencing can justifiably be used.

Street façade design should on the whole be restful or in the nature of a background to the activities of moving urban life; it should not obtrude itself into the scene. On level sites, horizontal lines and 'direction' and urbanity of character give repose. On sloping sites, the effect should be similar but the roof-line becomes an important factor, and the desired effect is perhaps best achieved by rhythmic, i.e. regular, stepping. Stepping can also be combined in the case of a curving street with a corresponding setting forward in units. Where streets slope steeply, assuming this to be unavoidable, while the carriageway must remain at an incline, the footways and pavings may be better arranged in a series of horizontal planes with steps and return ramps, at intervals thus providing level bases for the buildings. This is not only convenient but visually more satisfactory.

It is fitting that the degree of importance of a town street should be reflected by the buildings in type and design. A broad thoroughfare flanked by small mean hovels is a miserable sight, and a comparatively minor road-way bordered by great edifices is equally inappropriate if less unsightly.

Reverting to streets leading to and framing terminal features, the façades should not conflict in interest or an undesirable anticlimax will result. Sometimes there is no strong terminal feature to the street, it may be open at one or both ends, or lead to a non-accented building or to a return façade or to a space such as a square or gardens. Terminal interest can be created by a pronounced vertical feature at the end of one or other façades, e.g. a corner tower, but not at both ends or a conflict of interest or duality will result.

Street furniture

This is a term used to describe collectively the many minor, but mainly essential elements in urban design. They include such items as: light standards, electricity and telephone poles (cables would be better under-ground), traffic signs, refuges and beacons, post-boxes, litter-bins, street names and numbers, guard-rails, bollards and island refuges, pedestrian barriers, police-boxes, telephone call boxes, transformer substations, public toilets and other items.

Even when towns are well laid out and the buildings well designed, visual chaos or at least unpleasant eyesores can result from ill-placed or ugly elements of these kinds. In new developments, the siting or positioning should be considered from the outset, and the design of individual elements and their grouping – they can often be combined – should be a matter of regard for the overall visual effect as well as efficient function. The two aspects go together.

In existing towns, as many of the elements are the responsibility of different authorities or different government departments, there has often been a lack of co-ordination, with sorry results. All too often, the disposition has been as hazardous as it has been haphazard – duplication, obstruction of pavements, mutual obscuring and general unsightliness – some litter-bins are themselves visual litter! To clean up such a mess should be an urgent task of responsible town authorities. When elements can be specially designed, the basic factors of good design can be observed. But many of the elements have to be of standard designs, perhaps some for ease of recognition, for economic reasons have to be chosen from a limited range of available types. In the latter case choice should be governed by suitability of material, form and colour appropriate to the subject, its situation and the surroundings.

Light standards, while in the first instance they must be put at intervals for effective illumination, can by their placing in relation to buildings and roads contribute to the definition of the shapes of streets, squares or crescents.

Mention may also be made in this context of 'wirescape', the disfiguring cobwebbing of towns by overhead electricity and telephone cables, television aerials and the like, which are visually offensive. Existing cables should be re-routed or removed and greater control should be exercised in new developments.

Street signs

Street signs in a small way are examples of layout and microcosms of visual design. They are most important to the overall environmental effect.

The majority of signs are either (a) informative or (b) directive. Both kinds can include warnings. They may be free-standing or affixed to other structures, and can consist of metal, wood, glass, plastic or card, alone or in combination. They can be painted, printed, moulded, cast or carved, and may include lights and/or moving parts. The materials used and the methods of construction or manufacture should be the source of design characteristics.

Examples are:

(a) Informative. Town and village names; street names and numbers; shop names, fascias, hanging signs; names on buildings; traffic signs, e.g. parking place.
(b) Directional. Signposts, arrows; entrance, exit, etc.; traffic signs, e.g. keep left, diversion.
(c) Warning. Stop, danger; traffic-lights.

Signs, whether individually designed or selected from standard types must be efficient for the purpose for which they are intended and must be placed with regard to visibility. Attention should be paid particularly to legibility and the position, size and colours of lettering or symbols:

Recognition. – In many cases, use of standard lettering, symbol, shape or layout assists in immediate effectiveness in conveying message.
Brevity. The more detailed the message, the weaker the impact.

Coordinated range of furniture, including light standards, shelters, seats, traffic signs, telephone kiosks, barrier rails, etc. (above, arranged for exhibition purposes). Basic components are coated hollow rolled steel sections.

Double span bus shelter composed of units — steel framing with steel and glass panels (right). Glazing not only permits view of approaching transport but also reduces visual obstruction.

STREET FURNITURE

Examples of simple, efficient and visually acceptable standard designs.

Minimum number and size. Multiplicity of signs causes visual chaos and may result in dangerous distraction; related signs can often be combined on common mountings; signs should be as small as function allows (motorway signs are large because they have to be read at a distance by drivers travelling at speed.

Position. Must not obscure or be obscured; must be visually related to pavings or other ground elements; if affixed to walls or buildings they become part of architectural design and should conform thereto.

Good design can be furthered by (1) planning control; (2) co-operation of manufacturers and authorities in production of standard ranges of acceptable designs; (3) adoption of modular design, e.g. unit horizontal and vertical dimensions on which all signs are based.

Lettering

Letters and numerals are often a major part of street and other signs, some of which consist of little else. Unfortunately, the alphabets used are not always suitable. It is seldom necessary specially to design the characters as a wide range of acceptable types to meet all environmental needs already exists. It is selection that is important. Obvious considerations are: legibility – size, arrangement, colour, perhaps illumination; material – modification according to method of production; character – appropriate to subject.

The standard lettering used for traffic signs and at airports and railway-stations are good examples. Uniformity is desirable in repeated urban signing, e.g. street names and numbers within a defined area. Some variety is permissible for shop fascias seen in sequence provided they are on panels of standard size or are otherwise related.

Advertisements

Advertisements which are indiscriminately designed and placed can seriously mar the urban scene by their ugly, disruptive and distractive visual effect.

They are, however, necessary and provision should be planned so that they may be properly displayed.

The extent to which they are permitted in any area varies. Entertainment centres are likely to be where the greatest concentration can be allowed; residential districts the least.

From the advertiser's point of view, maximum prominence and attention focusing is the main object but clearly this aim must be subordinated to the overall design. There should be no conflict between advertisements and building form.

Limits of advertisements should be defined architecturally and the types of advertisement should be appropriate to their positions. A single advertisement that is unduly obtrusive is visually objectionable; multiple advertisements of such designs can cause visual chaos. The use of coloured lights, especially if intermittent, may be a source of danger along vehicular traffic routes because of confusion with traffic signals.

In Britain, the display of advertisements and advertising devices is fairly stringently controlled by restrictive legislation. The definitions of advertisements, which include hoardings and similar structures, are comprehensive, and the regulations set out where and under what conditions they can be displayed. In general, areas of special control are those where no advertisements are permitted, other areas are those where consent is required. This control has been effective in preventing the worst abuses of advertising on rural and urban scenes as found in some other countries.

Flyposting is a particularly unsightly kind of advertising; it is almost always a trespass and a prosecutable offence but appears to be less preventable.

Poster advertising

Posters are made of sheets of standard dimensions. Their overall size should be related to position, e.g. large posters for hoardings; smaller posters for pedestrian precincts, railway-stations, airports, etc., or anywhere where seen at close range. Illuminated drums of posters can be used with discretion, but preferably not centrally, in open and enclosed spaces.

10
Environmental Conditions

Local environment

The prime purpose of most buildings is to provide shelter and comfortable conditions for various activities and purposes. Comfort is achieved by climate modification:

1. by influencing the microclimate (climate about buildings);
2. by the design of the building envelope (walls, roof, etc. and insulation);
3. by control of internal conditions (heating, air-conditioning, etc.).

Meteorological or natural climate varies greatly in different parts of the world, and urban climate modification is at present less precise and effective than control within buildings, but the following notes indicate possibilities.

Temperature and humidity

These are two of the important factors upon which human comfort depends. They interact; temperature alone is not decisive – a high temperature with low humidity (relative humidity) may be more tolerable than a lower temperature with high humidity.

1. *Hot humid climate* (e.g. mainly tropical and sub-tropical areas such as South America, Central America, West Indies, India, Malaysia, but also Louisiana, and, in summer, New York City and Washington). Internal comfort is obtained by the use of fans, dehumidifying plant, full air-conditioning, but outside conditions can be mitigated and thereby internal measures assisted by planning provisions for:

(a) open layouts and orientation of buildings for maximum benefits from prevailing breezes and minimum effect of sun; locating of developments on high ground and hills, on sides of valleys; use of raised

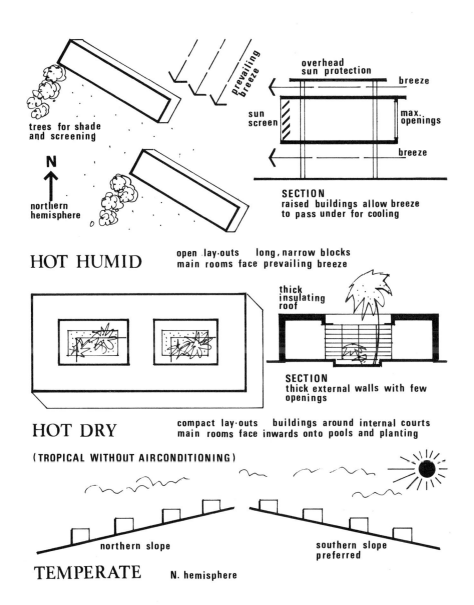

trees for shade and screening

N ↑

northern hemisphere

prevailing breeze

overhead sun protection

breeze

sun screen

max. openings

breeze

SECTION
raised buildings allow breeze to pass under for cooling

HOT HUMID
open lay-outs   long, narrow blocks
main rooms face prevailing breeze

thick insulating roof

SECTION
thick external walls with few openings

HOT DRY
compact lay-outs   buildings around internal courts
main rooms face inwards onto pools and planting

(TROPICAL WITHOUT AIRCONDITIONING)

northern slope

southern slope preferred

TEMPERATE   N. hemisphere

CLIMATE siting, lay·out, etc. examples

(open ground floor) and high rise buildings; inducement of air movement and avoidance of totally enclosed courts;

(*b*) planting and maintaining of grassed areas and massed trees. Vegetation loses heat quicker, minimises heat reflection and glare, and has cooling psychological effect.

2. *Hot dry climate* (e.g. Mexico, California, North Africa, Arabia, and, in summer, Spain and Italy. Often very hot during the day and very cold at night). Traditionally, buildings are compactly arranged within environmental areas and are grouped about closed courtyards (atrium, patio-type plans). Square plan forms having the least exposed external wall surfaces are used as opposed to long narrow blocks in a hot humid climate, but the internal use of air-conditioning permits freer arrangements of plans and arrangements. The use of loggias, pools or fountains, especially within courts, and planting in external open areas are desirable measures but are usually difficult to maintain.

3. *Temperate climate:* because of wide seasonal variations, temperature and humidity modification by planning are less important than other factors in design, but scientific investigations into microclimates of existing towns in the Northern Hemisphere indicate that:

(*a*) air temperature increases from the periphery to the centre of urban areas at rates according to structural densities. South-facing slopes have higher temperatures. Clear, stable weather conditions show the greatest temperature variations, whereas overcast conditions show the least, although urban temperatures are only slightly affected;

(*b*) air temperature over paved areas are higher than over grassed areas. The maximum difference is at dusk due to 'onset of night-time' cooling of the latter;

(*c*) there are 'heat islands'.

Generally, as solar radiation ceases in evening, temperature falls off in rural areas, but in urban areas temperature is maintained by released heat stored in the fabric of buildings, and by increased domestic and industrial heating and lighting, etc.

Summary:

(*a*) Rural areas and large grassed or planted areas have lower minimum temperatures with rapid responses to weather changes.

(*b*) Urban areas have higher minimum temperatures which increase with the structural density. Responses to weather or time of day are slower and therefore there is independence on them; there are however overall seasonal variations.

Interiors of air-conditioned buildings require protection from the sun. In the Telecommunications building (above) horizontal concrete louvres between structural frame shade equipment rooms, which have precisely controlled temperature and humidity.

The interior of the building (right) designed as multistorey department store, is protected from heat and glare by vertical aluminium sunbreakers of aerofoil section. Air conditioning plant for each floor is located behind contrasting travertine-faced solid walling.

CLIMATE
Air Conditioned
Buildings in the
Tropical Zone.

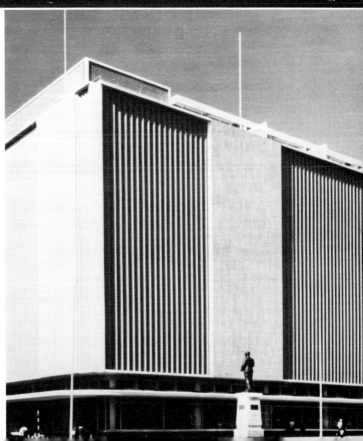

Microclimate

The benefits from a consistent urban microclimate are:

(*a*) reduction in cost of heating (or cooling) of buildings;
(*b*) reduction in costs of building maintenance by lessening of thermal movements;
(*c*) greater use of spaces in and around buildings.

To achieve these benefits, design considerations in regard to microclimate should include:

(*a*) orientation of buildings ⎫
(*b*) spacing of buildings ⎬ e.g. low-rise high-density developments on south-facing slopes will modify climate more effectively than similar developments on north-facing slopes, and still more efficiently than high-rise low-density buildings on either slope;
    (structural density) ⎭

(*c*) topographical location of buildings;
(*d*) constructional materials;

with the object of obtaining the best microclimate according to circumstances. Much more data is still required from more detailed investigations however, and from the correlation of other research, such as effects of air movement, for the establishment of reliable guide-lines for use in the environmental planning process.

Air movement

Air movement may be beneficial in improving climatic conditions but high winds can cause damage and loss of life.

High winds may occur in almost any part of the world but the risk is greater in some areas such as the tropics (hurricanes). Apart from constructional precautions in such areas consideration must be given to siting and laying out of buildings to minimise danger. Not only has direct pressure to be guarded against, but also suction and other vagaries.

At present, reliable data on which to base designs for such conditions is somewhat inadequate, but investigations continue in regard to high-rise (tall, isolated buildings) and low-rise estates (three-storey buildings and under) with the object of formulating design recommendations. Meantime, possible effects of air movement can be studied to some extent by the use of scale models in wind tunnels. Attention is also being paid to means of reducing unpleasant windy conditions in housing, shopping and other urban developments.

The prevailing wind in an area is not necessarily the strongest wind. Near the coast the strongest winds tend to blow from the sea. Hurricanes and similar storms are unpredictable in direction.

Shelter

Protection from high and persistent winds as a part of climate modification in exposed areas increases outdoor human comfort and mental activity and reduces psychological stress. For animals and crops, protection is provided in the form of planted trees and shrubs at right-angles to the direction of prevailing winds, and cover is given for game. Such screens should not be too near buildings, sports grounds or parks as although the provision of shelter is advantageous, if air movement is unduly impeded, stagnation can result. Advantages of shelter for buildings, alone or in groups, are : fuel bills are reduced, windows can be opened more often, and greater use can be made of the immediate surrounding space.

Design considerations : (a) shelter against strong winds and gales can be provided by broad belts of trees, closely spaced, low on windward side; (b) the breaking or reducing of the force of winds can be effected by narrow belts of single trees which need not necessarily be evergreens. In Britain, planting on the North and East gives protection against cold winds, but there are some parts of the country where protection against prevailing South-West winds is more important. Shelter planting is pleasing in itself and can contribute to general visual compositions as well as perform a valuable function.

Slow air movement, e.g. cold air which tends to flow into hollows and valleys can be deflected by planting at the upper level of such areas.

There are benefits from air movement as referred to previously in this chapter in regard to hot/humid climates. Also in the blowing away of industrial smoke, fumes and smells, and the general freshening of the atmosphere.

Consideration of wind velocities and directions are important in connection with the siting and layout of airports and harbours for operational reasons.

Sunlight, daylight and glare

It is generally accepted that buildings where people live and work should receive adequate daylight under average conditions, and that in temperate climes, habitable rooms in dwellings should receive some sunlight. This involves considerations of siting orientation and spacing, the latter so that one building does not unduly reduce the amount of light received by another. This can be controlled by reference to 'Daylight Indicators' which are used, in conjunction with permissible heights and floor space indices, to ensure adequate daylighting of buildings and of streets and other spaces between them, thus encouraging open types of developments, i.e. free-standing taller buildings rather than corridor streets with continuous façades along both sides. In practice, however, the result has often been podiums of two or three storeys with central towers. Recent research tends to show this is not the most efficient development. The cruciform arrangement is a more effective use of a square site. Many other factors influence building form and undue adherence to daylighting theory can result in rigid geometrical layouts. Daylight controls alone are not now regarded as satisfactory regulators. The use of artificial light in combination with daylight has become an established technique for commercial buildings, referred to as PSALI – Permanent Supplementary Artificial Lighting of Interiors – which reduces dependence on conventional fenestration. Indeed, some offices and factories now rely wholly on artificial lighting.

Tropical conditions. The foregoing notes refer to temperate climes but in the tropics and hot, sunny regions generally the problem is not of ensuring sufficient natural light but of shielding interiors from excessive light and glare, especially in the early mornings and the later afternoons. These are building design problems for which many solutions exist, but some, e.g. the use of external shielding devices such as louvres, fins, canopies, greatly affect the appearance of buildings.

Environmental noise

Sound is perceived by hearing – vibrations through the ear. Vibration is experienced by feeling – rapid movements to and fro. Noise is an unpleasant and disturbing sound, harmful physically and psychologically, especially to the sick; it interferes with concentration, reduces efficiency, causes mental distress.

The main sources of noise in the environment are:

road vehicles and traffic;
airports and aircraft;
roadworks and building construction;
industry, especially heavy industry;
railways and ships.

Vibrations can be measured extremely finely and techniques concerning sound and the science of acoustics are among the most advanced, yet noise, which is part of the daily assault on the senses, is one of the major if not most serious of atmospheric pollutions. Of the sources listed, the worst in the sense of the most widespread and most persistent is traffic noise. The extent of traffic noise results from the numbers and types of vehicles, speeds, gradients, road surfaces, and local environmental and climatic conditions. There are methods of defining traffic noise – TNI – traffic noise index – and it has been suggested that a vehicle could be rated or weighted according to its effect on the environment, e.g. EPCU – Environmental Passenger Car

Unit – an extension of PCU which is used for traffic stream calculations. A motor-cycle would be rated 3EPCU (three times as much noise as an ordinary passenger car) rather than 0.67PCU, its relative size.

Two courses of action in regard to traffic and other noises are possible:

1. Eliminate or reduce at source – legislation and planning.
2. Minimise or mitigate effect – siting, insulation and design of buildings.

1. At present, legislation appears ineffective; for example, motor-cyclists making excessive noise are seldom prosecuted or even warned.

Planning action should be the keeping of heavily-trafficked roads well away from dwellings and offices because noise, and poisonous fumes and dirt, diminish with distance. A formula to relate volume EPCU to distance might be established for design purposes in this respect.

2. The siting of buildings at right-angles to roads, with no windows on the road side, results in worthwhile noise reduction regardless of distance and ground attenuation, although this may conflict with other requirements. The avoidance of openings near internal angles is essential.

Insulation or screening, the provision of a physical barrier between the source of noise and the building can be achieved by: placing the road at lower level in a cutting; providing an intervening mound or embankment; planting of close foliage trees, which also act as dust filter; various kinds of walling; placing of less important buildings, such as store sheds or rooms to screen more important buildings or rooms.

Building design includes the use of air-conditioning, that is, mechanical heating, cooling and ventilating, in combination with double windows, not for climatic reasons, but to reduce outside noise for offices. This method is not yet usual for dwellings but they too can be similarly planned to reduce effects of noise.

Traffic vibration. Road traffic vibration is mainly transmitted through the ground and affects foundations causing structural damage to older buildings, especially historic structures, and interferes with various activities and processes, such as laboratory work with sensitive instruments, as well as causing general disturbance.

Remedial measures:

1. legislation – by restriction on types, sizes, weights, speeds of vehicles and prohibitions in some places;
2. planning – by the routing of roads and the siting of buildings as for noise reduction;
3. engineering – by suitable road construction, gradients, pavings;
4. building design – by isolation of foundations by means of trenches, and by the insulation of structural elements.

Airport and aircraft noise. The increase in size of jet aircraft, the pending introduction of supersonic transport, and the frequency of flights has produced major noise, vibration and sonic boom problems. There is a serious conflict between the needs of air traffic and the preservation of amenities; between the need for expanding existing airports and for establishing new airports, and the keeping of noise and disturbance within tolerable limits, conserving the countryside and preserving good agricultural land. Legislation can mitigate noise by governing permissible levels, angle of climb and avoidance of flights over residential areas, but as regards the siting of new airports, this is an example where integrated national planning is essential because of the size and extent of area affected, and the many existing land uses and potential future developments that are concerned. Siting of new airports on estuaries, where this is operationally feasible and within reasonable limits of cost, is a possible solution. In all cases it is necessary to prepare a comprehensive regional development scheme centred about the site chosen initially on bases of functional, operational and environmental considerations. A positive approach could lead to the enrichment and improvement of that region to offset whatever loss might be caused; some loss must always result.

Roadworks and construction noise. Earthmoving and pile-driving equipment, heavy construction traffic, excavators, mixers and mechanical plant of all kinds cause serious noise and often vibration problems, as well as dust and mud, but this is localised and although bad while it lasts is temporary. The nuisance can usually be confined to certain times of day.

Industrial noise. Considerable noise, along with other undesirable pollutions, is generated by heavy industrial plants and undertakings, such as extractive plants, steelworks, shipbuilding, etc. Locations are usually predetermined by other considerations, and therefore vulnerable developments should be planned away from such sites.

Railways and shipping noises. These have been largely accepted and are not regarded as serious nuisances up to the present, but future high speed rail transport and increased underground services, now used in most large cities in the world, and possibility of new types of elevated railways, will require careful consideration of noise and vibration aspects.

The foregoing refers to 'outside' noise. Noise can also be generated within and about dwellings. Although on a lower scale, it can be a source of annoyance to neighbours. Siting of dwellings for adequate daylight and air is generally sufficient to prevent undue disturbance. Thereafter, it becomes a matter of building design using physical means of reducing sound transmission.

11
Building Design and Constructional Technology

Buildings and other artefacts comprise the greater part of the visual urban environment, so it is necessary to know the structural systems and constructional methods which are, or should be, the bases of form and outward appearance. These systems and methods give physical implementation to functional requirements and conversely influence them.

Changes in external design result as much from constructional technological advances as from new or varied functional requirements, and much more than from any individual designer's influence except when that designer is, in fact, appreciating and exploiting inevitable change.

First, a brief review of structural systems:

1. *Trabeated* – weight-bearing wall/post and beam; that is, vertical supports and horizontal beams. A simple, but limited system, used almost exclusively in the ancient world, e.g. Egypt, Greece.
2. *Arcuated* – the arch and its derivatives, domes and vaults. The arch is a curved arrangement of wedged-shaped units or of joints between units, requiring temporary support until complete. It enables considerable spans to be bridged, large clear spaces to be covered. A system exploited by the Romans, and the basis of subsequent Byzantine, Romanesque and Gothic styles of architecture.
3. *Framed* – consisting essentially of a structural framework of thin members joined together supporting non-structural panels, e.g. in primitive times a web of branches covered by animal skins or wattle and daub; the medieval half-timber and noggin; modern timber buildings; multi-storey steel skeletons; and more recent developments such as space frames, geodesic domes, cable suspensions and networks.
4. *Monolithic* – this system virtually results from and is confined to reinforced concrete, which makes possible many and ingenious ways

117

of enclosing and covering space including large clear areas, and the use of geometrical curvatures of many kinds with considerable range of combinations and interpenetrations. Unit plastic construction is on similar lines but is much smaller in scale.

5. *Flexible inflated* – this system has limited applications and is used for temporary structures. Sometimes described as *pneumatic*.

Each system has distinctive design characteristics which should be apparent in form and shape.

Historically, in western Europe, prior to the Renaissance, buildings almost always clearly revealed their structural systems but, notwithstanding the awakened interest in scientific structural investigation and progress in construction skills and in spatial manipulation, separation then began between function/structure and outward appearance. However, because of the relative simplicity of practical requirements, because construction materials were few and localised due to difficulties of transport, and because methods were largely dependent upon human labour, although classical trappings were much used, these circumstances imposed a discipline, and many buildings of this period have an orderly charm and distinction of design, especially the less grandiose, in which the manner of their planning and construction is not unduly obscured.

This is observed in buildings of the seventeenth and eighteenth centuries in Britain. However, the nineteenth century in Britain was a period of enormous advances in constructional technology resulting from the mechanical and industrial revolutions, the effects of urban growth, and new discoveries of power and their utilisation. Mass production and distribution of traditional building materials, adaptation of power units coupled to mechanical devices, and scientific investigation into and application of structural principles, increasingly expanded constructional possibilities and achievements in the use of cement, concrete, reinforced concrete, steel sections – frames, lattice grids, arches, trusses – glass, ceramics, sanitary fittings and pipes, imported timbers, mechanical plant for heating and ventilating, plus piped water supply, main drainage, electric light and power, lifts and many others.

Unfortunately, this expansion of constructional technology with its great potential for building and urban design coincided with a widening gap between function/structure and outward appearance, which ought to be related and integrated aspects of total design. Buildings were clothed in period costume of all kinds, an eclecticism mightily encouraged by literary effusions. A few utilitarian structures were honourable exceptions. This design attitude continued into the twentieth century but functional requirements, including services and climatic control, had become so complex, and

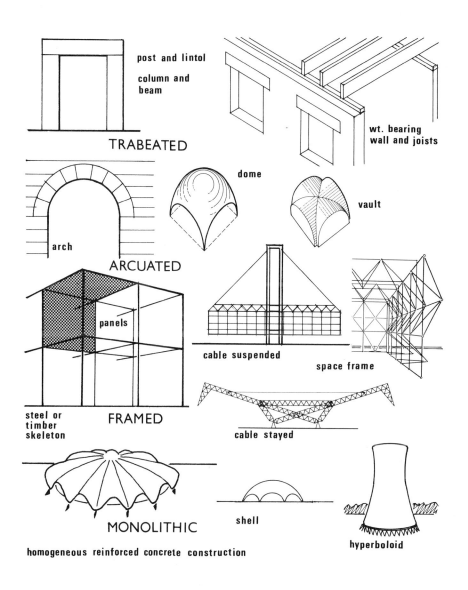

post and lintol
column and
beam

TRABEATED

wt. bearing
wall and joists

dome

vault

arch

ARCUATED

panels

cable suspended

space frame

steel or
timber
skeleton

FRAMED

cable stayed

MONOLITHIC

shell

hyperboloid

homogeneous reinforced concrete construction

STRUCTURAL SYSTEMS
main types and examples

technical advances were so powerful and the ugliness, disorder and visual chaos so manifest, that a new approach to the design of buildings and the planning of towns had to come. After initial confusion and the pursuit of various 'isms', building design is increasingly recognised and accepted, so also is urban design, as a logical process with well-defined principles. These principles determine functional requirements, and constructional possibilities and limitations, whatever prevailing conditions exist.

Today, technology continues to advance to cope more efficiently with new complex practical, psychological and social needs in a time of general change and transition. New ways of using traditional materials are developed and new materials made available : stainless steel and non-ferrous metals and alloys, asbestos cement products, plastics of various kinds, laminates, cladding, etc. These materials, together with new fixings and finishes, and new constructional design methods inescapably affect the outward form and surface appearance of buildings and urban development. Standardisation and prefabrication were used to a limited extent for a long time but are now widely adopted especially for larger elements, in conjunction with modular and dimensional co-ordination, industrialised and system building methods, computerisation – to provide information retrieval, component selection and detailed drawing production – coding and data co-ordination. This tends to restrict the number of types and sizes of components – that is indeed the object in order to reduce cost – but new inventions and discoveries continue to widen designers' choice. Construction has become to considerable extent an industry, adopting factory production and management techniques ; this applies especially to site organisation.

In the future, in the production of dwellings and other repetitive plan construction, e.g. apartments or hotel suites, units complete with wiring and services, all ready for dropping on to prepared supports ōr for stacking will be common, use being made of one-piece plastic and other synthetic materials formed by power press extrusions.

The present lines of development cannot be reversed. With overpopulation the most serious problem of today, there is no alternative to such mass production to provide adequate accommodation : houses, flats, schools, hospitals, economically in the quantities needed.

Although inevitable repetition of standard designs, having no affinity with local conditions, could have visual staleness and be deficient in some qualities, these defects can be compensated for by : imaginative layouts and groupings, use of landscaping and planting, careful selection of colours, and introduction of well-chosen, well-designed incidental items. The object, as always, is the creation of an orderly, visually attractive, as well as efficient environment by co-operation between planners, urban designers and architects.

12
Preservation and Conservation

It is generally accepted in most countries that the preservation of buildings of architectural merit or historic interest is of cultural value and, in some cases, makes economic good sense, when the buildings can have continued worthwhile use and are tourist attractions. Legislation protects such buildings to some extent, but opinions often vary as to worthiness in individual instances. Although financial grants may be available, costs of repair, renovation, and of subsequent maintenance are factors that have to be taken into account. Preservation of buildings merely because they are old have vague historical connections, or for sentimental or nostalgic reasons, is unrealistic.

Apart from major archaeological remains, fragments of antiquity, and 'ancient monuments', sound reasons for preservation apply to:

1. buildings and structures of any era which are the earliest or among the earliest of their kinds or are good examples of important design developments, providing they are reasonably intact or capable of effective, sensitive restoration, especially those exhibiting exceptional integrity of design of fabric, interiors and setting. These buildings are, in the best sense, 'museum pieces' and should be furnished and maintained accordingly;
2. buildings that are of architectural stylistic interest and are in good condition, capable of adaptation for continued use by means of internal alterations and unobtrusive provision of services;
3. buildings as (2), but although of little interest individually, may with others have group value and are deemed worthy of inclusion in conservation areas, as referred to later in this chapter.

Buildings and structures with strong associations with historical persons or events may be included in any of the above categories.

Treatment of individual buildings in relation to the environment

Many buildings worthy of preservation exist in isolation, that is, they stand in their own grounds or are surrounded by roads. Planning control should ensure that they are not encroached upon. Others, especially in central urban situations, although originally free-standing, have had later buildings abutting, probably of different scale, materials and character causing visual detriment. If possible in such cases, the later buildings and accretions should be removed so that the original building is again visually isolated and can be seen from all sides.

Some buildings, however, have only one façade of importance, and it would be wrong to expose its sides. But there should be provided a clear vertical dividing 'line', such as a narrow recessed plain strip, between the façade and adjoining buildings, which should preferably be simple in treatment and in keeping in character and scale, although not necessarily in style.

Sometimes it happens that a low building of a past age, which has escaped destruction or mutilation by reason of its nature, e.g. an almshouse, has or could become surrounded by multi-storey office blocks. The resultant great contrast of size and scale can be turned to advantage if the foregoing principle of visual isolation or separation is observed. Advance planning could ensure a reasonable space around the preserved building, but where this is no longer possible, then a surrounding wall of appropriate design or boundary trees or other means of 'framing' can be used. Such setting apart enables disparate buildings of special interest to be happily incorporated in the environment and provides added interest in the clearly defined comparison of the old and the new.

Buildings of particular importance in category (1) above could literally be placed in a 'glass case' or a plastic panelled geodesic dome, so that by weather protection and controlled temperature and humidity, decay and otherwise inevitable deterioration could be arrested.

Conservation areas

As well as the preservation of individual buildings, planning legislation usually provides for the preservation of groups of buildings and their related environment in what are known as conservation areas. Such areas are of various kinds and extent. Architectural style may be the main consideration, e.g. an eighteenth-century square or a Regency terrace; or it may be an informal arrangement of buildings of different periods or of general townscape as in an unspoiled village, into which uncontrolled and incongruous new developments would be visually objectionable. Legislation aims, however, not at prohibiting any new development – to do so might well cause further neglect and decay — but at promoting satisfactory development that not only accords with the qualities of the areas in the environmental sense but that will assist in maintaining or in regenerating social amenities and economic prosperity. This approach not only preserves what is there, but utilises the potential. To do so is not always easy. Old buildings, even if structurally sound, often require expensive repairs and alterations to meet present-day standards of accommodation and services and to eliminate fire risks. If grants or other funds are insufficient or not available, future economic viability needs careful investigation. Some buildings, presentable on front façades are badly decayed at the rear with unsightly additions over original open space; this may present opportunities for providing service roads, car parks, and possibly new housing and other buildings. Where the façades are urban 'stage sets', as many Renaissance buildings are, and where the rear is severely blighted, it might be best to construct completely new buildings behind the fronts.

The following are general suggestions for the treatment of Conservation Areas:

1. make careful initial survey to establish age and condition, environmental qualities, etc.;
2. remove, so far as practicable, unsuitable and incongruous buildings and structures;
3. discontinue inappropriate uses;
4. remove alien features, ugly and superfluous signs; as regards advertisements, define as 'area of special control', but if they are not unseemly, well-designed, well-placed advertisements may be permitted as they add interest and vitality;
5. restore and clean masonry, repair woodwork, repaint in acceptable colours — usually as originally, but sometimes brighter colours are permissible;
6. replace any unsatisfactory fascias and lettering with good design; fascias are often too deep, irregular and in unpleasant colours with ugly and illegible lettering;
7. modernise or reconstruct interiors, except where they are of architectural interest and quality; promote new developments appropriate in uses and harmonious in character, scale, materials and colours, but former styles should not be copied unless it is necessary to restore or maintain a unity of appearance which previously existed. Other gaps may well be filled if visual composition so requires but care is needed to ensure a satisfactory effect from all possible points of view; it is not sufficient to consider one aspect only; there must be skilful interlacing of new with old; uses of areas should be related to social framework and overall planning;

8. in streets and spaces, remove obsolescent lighting fittings and replace with good designs; in narrow streets and alleys hang fittings from buildings to avoid congestion; conceal switchgear or make it unobtrusive; limit or prohibit vehicular traffic; form pedestrian precincts; ban motor-cycles, mopeds and heavy lorries; permit at most only sufficient traffic to give life and provide essential servicing; impose speed limits to walking pace. The objects of these measures are to prevent or minimise environmental disturbance, noise, fumes and 'severance'; also remove superfluous traffic or other signs and seek modification of regulations in regard to traffic signs and road markings on grounds of amenity;

9. landscape and floorscape: retain existing trees except where mutilated beyond restoration; plant new trees, provide shrub boxes and flower containers; lay out open spaces as appropriate: provide new pavings and street furniture; pedestrianisation in particular requires floorscape treatment.

13
Landscape Design

Landscape design is relevant to both the functional and the visual aspects of planning and urban design. Landscape in the environmental context refers to the laying out and planting of trees, shrubs, grass, etc., together with the provision of related features in open spaces from the smallest courtyard to large parks and even extensive tracks of countryside. Design includes the treatment of industrial installations and the rehabilitation of derelict and blighted areas and of mineral workings.

Land, water and organic life are used to satisfy human needs for outdoor activities and visual appreciation of natural beauty. But, unlike buildings and roads which are made from more or less inert materials, the elements from which much of landscaping is composed, move and change and grow with time and with weather, climate and the changing seasons.

Planners, urban designers and building designers have to know the fundamentals of landscape design, but detailed design is the work of specialists known as landscape architects, who are contributors to the design teams from the early stages of scheme formulation to final implementation – and beyond, as proper and continuing maintenance of landscaped areas is essential.

The scope of landscape design covers such matters as : ground modelling by grading and earth moving ; site drainage ; layouts, taking into account future growth ; general planting, e.g. grassed areas and ground cover ; tree planting for amenity and for particular purposes such as wind breaks ; screening and enclosure plantings and constructions ; microclimatic modification ; water features, e.g. lakes, pools, canals, reservoirs, fountains, waterfalls and cascades, water plants ; provision of hard surfaces, i.e. pavings, roads and footways ; provision of outdoor fittings and furniture, e.g. seats, plant containers, lamps and lighting, floodlighting of ground and trees ; litter-bins, signs and lettering, etc. ; fences, railings and bollards ; conservation and maintenance.

Basic information required in connection with any project includes:

1. contoured site survey and surroundings
2. climate and microclimate conditions
3. nature of soil and geological substrata
4. ecological conditions
5. visual character and potential

} these are obtained by investigation and research.

6. planning factors: (a) relation to other developments
   (b) effect on environment
   (c) influence on traffic
   (d) legal and other restrictions

} from consultation with planners and other specialists.

7. costs: initial and maintenance;
8. time factor and programming – seasonal and climatic conditions affect planting.

Uses of foregoing:

1. *Site contours* – for larger spaces, study may suggest best development of site as regards: ground modelling, drainage, positions of buildings and roads including the placing of under- and over-passes, location of car parks, retention and exploiting of views.
2. *Climate* – creation of favourable microclimate by site manipulation and planting of shelter belts.
3. *Nature of soil* – determining factor in selecting trees, plants and grass and in deciding planting policy in 'poor' areas and whether or not soil improvement is feasible; subsoil may be exposed by cuttings or modelling and nature will influence treatment; water table is also a design factor.
4. *Existing vegetation* – if suitable, may remain undisturbed; healthy trees should always be preserved; this may influence layout of buildings and roads.
5. *Water* – existing sources have to be investigated for purity, seasonal variation, flooding, if possible use for pools is contemplated, for water features and for drainage.
6. *Site surroundings* – these influence visual design: views seen from the site affect the placing of buildings and arrangement of planting as the screening of unpleasant sights may be necessary; conversely good views can be enhanced; views into site also to be considered. Barrier planting may be required to insulate against noise or dust, from neighbouring sources, and for security reasons.
7. *Urban factors* – existing or anticipated densities: people, buildings, traffic; social and economic conditions; behaviour characteristics;

Integrated trees and flower beds add to amenities and visual interest of seaside resort development . . .

LANDSCAPED SPACES

and to well-designed industrial estate

trees may be the dominant element in low-rise housing; urban parks, which may be linear, e.g. along rivers or streams, or designed as elements of definition around land/use zones. Parks are places for games and sports, casual walking, picnicking and general enjoyment of open air in pleasant surroundings; they should have spacious grassed areas with added interest of trees, mounds, water, not over-elaborate but arranged for economic maintenance.

General design principles

Basic principles of landscape design are the same as those that apply to planning and architecture; layouts or arrangements have to satisfy practical and functional requirements. After these have been analysed and assessed, both initially and as modified during design procedure, physical imple-mentation follows by selecting and manipulating organic and constructional elements. The composition is developed in combination with existing build-ings and other structures and any natural features and surroundings and fully integrates them. Absence of a formal pattern, except for incidental pavings, screen walls and similar constructions, is desirable. Not only is regularity of spacing, exact repetition of types and arrangements, and uni-formity of size and shape contrary to natural growth, it lessens the value of contrast, which is so important a function of landscaping in most cases. However, there is a case for orderly arrangements of appropriate species of trees as avenues and for balancing areas of planting and other features in association with important buildings and urban squares. This reinforces the impression of dignity and special significance, and focuses interest on approaches, entrances, monuments. But, informality is not 'wildness'. Landscaping is controlled nature, and control must be maintained. In urban spaces and in the proximity of buildings, and in a progressively less extent towards the open countryside, regular cutting of grass, weeding, trimming and pruning – but not 'butchery'! – and, re-seeding and re-planting, as necessary, should be provided for.

Summing up: landscape design must be efficient in its functional role, as part of the overall plan, in the provision of pleasant open spaces for physical rest and recreation and psychological relief, in the provision of visual contrast, while being complementary, to buildings and roads, and by the provision of visual satisfaction in the enjoyment of natural beauty.

Conservation of areas of natural beauty

As the value to the public of national parks, inland and coastal amenity areas and country parks lies in their natural state, the existing landscape qualities must be preserved while permitting reasonable access. This may mean the continuance of farming and grazing, and acceptable afforestation,

LANDSCAPED
SHOPPING CENTRE

Pool with fountain, trees casting dappled shadows, varied pavings, and open clock tower feature contribute to interesting and pleasant central space in shopping precinct.

Horrible example of trees in residential street. The severe treatment (left) in Spring results in unnatural growth (right) in Summer. The footway completely blocked for several weeks!

with protection of existing flora and fauna. Means of preservation must not defeat the essential object. Within the areas, public use must be unobtrusively guided and controlled by skilful directional planting with a minimum use of carefully placed, appropriately designed, signposts and fencing in traditional materials; planned picnic areas and facilities of various kinds among trees or in hollows; paths left as grass tracks unless soil or heavy traffic necessitates simple gravelling, avoiding kerbs or straight lines; regular clearance of litter and sometimes warden patrols against vandalism. Screened perimeter car parks should be provided at approaches where vehicular access would be an intrusion.

14
Maintenance

The achievement of good design in the planning of the environment and in individual buildings as a worthy objective is generally recognised, but less understood and appreciated is the need for constant maintenance. Dirt, decay and accretions of one kind or another, the results of neglect, can quickly and seriously mar and ultimately destroy the values of the finest layouts and urban designs.

There are two groups of problems in most areas: (1) the existing accumulated dereliction of the past, and (2) the failure to cope adequately with repairs and cleaning, and the taking of preventative measures, in the present.

Maintenance of towns, buildings and roads

Means of eliminating or minimising the effects of time, weather, destructive organisms, and wear (if not abuse) should be considered at the design stage. There is now ample evidence from observation and research as to how constructional failures, staining, soiling, deterioration and damage are caused, and regard should be paid in the arrangement of elements, methods of assembly, and choice of materials, surface treatments, etc., to prevent or reduce these known risks. However, it is not possible, even without the limitations of economic constraints, to obtain a completely maintenance-free environment. Therefore, constant vigilance and repetitive attention are necessary, and the upkeep of layouts, roads, buildings and all structures in the visual as well as the practical sense must be regarded as a joint responsibility of owners, occupiers and the public through local authorities.

In the majority of municipal organisations there would seem to be a missing man – or perhaps a missing woman – whose job it would be, as it should in any civilised community, to travel about, observing and receiving reports, and then to instigate remedial action in regard to the minor actual and visual pollutions that detract from satisfactory environmental design at every turn : the tumble-down walls and fences, unkept gardens, torn and defaced posters, obsolete electioneering and other graffiti (what sane person would vote for anyone whose supporters scrawl slogans on walls, pavements and even trees !), missing letters from street signs and building names, worn, weed and litter strewn grassed and planted spaces and 'left-over' corners, broken lamps, bent railings and so on.

But powers do exist in most countries under Planning and Housing Acts for dealing with slums, insanitary dwellings and property in bad repair. There are also provisions for the prevention of dumping of refuse and abandoned vehicles, and for the improvement of aptly but unfortunately named 'waste' land if conditions seriously affect amenity. Action arising from such legislation can assist in maintaining a tolerable environment, and can gradually wipe out the worst of the inherited eyesores in the urban scene, and replace them by well-designed layouts and buildings.

Reclamation and rehabilitation

Away from towns, considerable areas of land have been laid waste by the industrial operations of earlier times when such spoilation was thought to be an inevitable concomitant. These now derelict mineral workings, gravel-pits, spoil heaps and tips, and lands rendered sterile by chemicals and poisonous substances, can only be retrieved in many instances by long and difficult effort, which, although regarded as uneconomic at present, may well become necessary and urgent in the near future as the need for land becomes pressing, quite apart from amenity considerations. That reclam-ation is possible using modern techniques is the important thing, and it should therefore be progressively employed so that the areas can be made usable again and in some cases can become a source of visual pleasure.

The task, which falls within the sphere of activities of the landscape architect, requires expert understanding and application of ecological and biological processes, so that natural balance can be adjusted and all uses and functions integrated for continuing growth and improvement. In some parts there can be a return to agriculture or forestry; in others, excavations can be made into artificial lakes for fishing and boating with the surround-ings turned into parks for rest, recreation and leisure pursuits; and some may be utilised for properly planned and designed building develop-ments.

As regards present-day industrial workings, it is now the responsibility, ensured by legislation, of the undertakings concerned to make good after extractions and other disturbances, e.g. by removal of topsoil at the outset and its return after appropriate filling and/or ground modelling, and to dispose of slag, ash and similar waste material in an acceptable manner, and they must budget accordingly. Such restoration of land should be planned in advance, and this also requires expert advice.

Appendix

Verbal design assessments

In the preceding chapters explanations of basic aspects of design in the built environment have been given, and a number of principles and their practical applications have been described. It has not been possible to cover every type of development nor to go into great detail in every respect, but the examples that have been mentioned should serve to indicate the various general considerations to be taken into account in the design process.

In conclusion, an attempt is made to outline a simple method of objectively assessing visual environmental design, both as a means of judging completed works and of evaluating proposals and projects. The method suggested is that of verbal assessment to describe satisfactory or unsatisfactory features of a design against a check list, using everyday words, of which the meanings are commonly understood.

A comprehensive list could be drawn up to include planning, urban design and building design, or separate lists, appropriately modified, could be prepared for each of these three divisions of the environment, although each would include reference to the other two.

A list alone can be a valuable means of considering a design, but the conscious correlation of agreed words on an item by item basis will pinpoint weaknesses or defects which otherwise might remain unperceived or be only vaguely felt. The method does not go, nor needs to go, beyond the main principles, nor does it pretend to measure exactly merits or demerits of a design. It does not deal with subtleties and ultra refinements. But it is important to get priorities in the right order and to consider the whole and major parts of design before details. No amount of fashionable ornamentation can excuse fundamental visual inadequacies. What the method can do is to distinguish between what is visually acceptable and what is not, without imposing rules or codes or otherwise hampering designers, who should always have the greatest possible freedom within the stated principles to exploit new ideas and new materials.

Assuming that the purely practical needs of function and use are satisfactory and that construction is sound and economic within prevailing circumstances, the following is a suggested basis for visual acceptability.

Visual effects of the environment

Check list	Acceptable	Not acceptable
planning layouts	orderly unified homogeneous integrated comprehensible	disorganised uncoordinated muddled confused incoherent
buildings as above plus structures	functionally and structurally expressive	functionally and structurally falsified disguised, faked
overall composition	clear and uncluttered well-arranged grouped focused concentrated interesting	chaotic fragmented dispersed diffused scattered commonplace
colours	harmonious (with judicious contrast) related suitable	gaudy, garish drab conflicting inappropriate
texture and pattern	functionally and structurally derived definite significant	arbitrarily imposed vague indiscriminate meaningless
proportion as above plus forms and shapes	simple consistent rhythmic	complex irrational random

Check list	*Acceptable*	*Not acceptable*
scale	correct reasonable	mean (too small) grandiose (too big)
details	appropriate fitting	incongruous
character (civic and public) (residential) (offices, industry) (entertainment)	positive dignified, distinguished attractive efficient, stimulating bright, cheerful, exciting	negative ordinary dreary squalid, depressing tawdry, humdrum
general use	clean tidy crisp well-kept seemly	dirty messy fussy neglected freakish

These or similar words honestly applied may help in encouraging a disciplined objective way of looking at the environment, and thus lead to common action in improving its design.

Glossary

The meaning of most words in the foregoing chapters should be clear from their contexts; others are explained. However, the following reference may be helpful in further clarifying the meanings of certain words and terms as used in this book.

Accents. Small elements which by form, shape, projection or colour are points of emphasis or attraction in a design.

Aesthetic. Synonym for subjective visual beauty – see Chapter 1.

Air-conditioning. Mechanical and artificial means of controlling temperature and humidity in a building.

Amenity. Anything that primarily contributes to physical and psychological pleasure.

Analysis. The breaking down into parts for separate study and/or classification.

Angle of Repose. The slope at which earth or any loose material normally becomes stable.

Artefact. Anything made or constructed by humans.

Architect (Building). A designer of buildings in detail.

Architect (Landscape). A specialist in the design of earthworks, parks, gardens, planted areas and ancillary works.

Aspect. View in a particular direction; the side of a building facing such a direction, e.g. south aspect.

Axis. A line, usually imaginary, about which a layout, a building, or a part of a building is symmetrically arranged.

Breaks. Relatively small changes in direction on plan or elevation.

Brief. A statement defining the objects which a design is required to fulfil – see Chapter 2.

Building. A physical enclosure of space or spaces for protection and other uses.

Built Environment. Man-made or man-organised physical surroundings to human activities – see Chapter 1.

Camber. A slight curvature, e.g. a road surface or underside of a beam.

Civil Engineer. A specialist designer of such structures as roads, bridges, harbours and associated works.

Cognoscente. One who is – or likes to think he is! – 'in the know'.

Coherent. Easily appreciated visually by reason of consistency and compatibility, i.e. everything obviously belonging together.

137

Conjoined. Combined; united.

Conservation (Buildings). Preservation of associated buildings by putting to new uses or incorporating in new developments.

Conservation (Land). Preservation in existing state by prevention of undesirable developments.

Contrived. Brought about regardless of visual effect or honesty of expression.

Cosmetic Treatment. Improvement of appearance of buildings and other structures by repairs, renovations and covering up of ugliness and defects; sometimes referred to as 'face lifting'.

Cost-efficiency. Value assessment taking into account cost in relation to efficient functional performance and durability.

Criterion. Standard of judgement.

Daylight Indicators. Angle controls for establishing permissible heights of buildings in relation to surrounding streets and near-by buildings to ensure adequate daylighting to the new buildings and to prevent undue diminution of daylight received by existing buildings and streets.

Definition. The clear demarkation of parts of a layout or of a building design by 'lines', breaks, or abrupt changes of colour or texture.

Design. The intentional putting together and/or shaping of materials to meet requirements or needs – see Chapter 1.

Developments. Any constructions on or uses of land areas.

Direction. Eye movement when applied to layouts and buildings: instruction in respect of signs.

Electicism. The taking of elements and stylistic details from various unrelated sources and embodying them in a design.

Ecology. The study of relationships between living organisms, vegetable and animal, and their surroundings.

Expression. The clear indication in the external appearance of a building of its functional planning and construction.

Enclave. Layout or group of buildings set apart from others.

Environmental Area. An area of development defined by distributor roads, and having no extraneous, i.e. non-essential, traffic.

Façade. Any side of a building facing on to a street or open space.

Feedback. Experience which is potentially of value in connection with new designs.

Fenestrated. Provided with windows.

Floorscape. Compositions consisting of pavings, level plantings and other more or less horizontal external areas.

Floor Space Index (FSI). The area of the total floor space of a building or buildings on a particular site divided by the area of site, including half the area of any adjoining roads; used as a means of controlling building density.

Form. Three-dimensional appearance of buildings or any objects – see Chapter 5.

Formwork. Temporary supports and moulds for casting concrete.

Hierarchy. Successive grades; order of importance or size.

Humidity. The amount of moisture in the atmosphere.

Impose. Arbitrarily to apply a surface or other treatment to a building or structure regardless of its purpose or construction.

Isolation. The separation or setting apart of a building or group of buildings by either open space or marked physical features.

Landscape. The natural scene, e.g. the countryside; but also applies to extensive grassed and planted areas, and laid out open spaces.

Landscaping. Refers to the treatment of surroundings to buildings and other structures by means of earthworks, organising of existing natural features, new planting of trees, shrubs and flowers, and pavings primarily for amenity; the word is also used rather absurdly, but not in this book, in connection with open plan interiors in which some potted plants are disposed.

Landscape Architect. See Architect.

Line. In building design, the outlines, edge and junctions of surfaces, joints and any long thin projections and recesses – see Chapter 5.

Manipulation. The adjustment of form, shape, line, colour and texture in designs with the objects of improving efficiency and/or appearance while retaining honesty of expression of function and structure.

Microclimate. Localised climate; climatic conditions immediately around and within a town or group of buildings.

Monumental. Large or grand buildings or structures, usually of symmetrical design; extensive layouts of similar characteristics.

Nodes. Focal-points in a layout, from which roads radiate or, conversely, at which they converge.

Norms. Usual standard types.

Orientation. (1) Relation of layout or building to points of compass, e.g. facing north; running east–west. (2) Coherent and comprehensible arrangement of a town – see Chapter 5.

Pedestrianisation. An ugly word meaning the converting of a road or other area for the sole use of pedestrians.

Pigment. A colouring agent.

Planner – Physical. A person concerned with the practical laying out of areas of land use, roads and other communications.

Planning. The laying out of land and the making of an efficient and pleasant environment for human needs and activities.

Pragmatic. Making use of available materials, skills and knowledge.

Prospect. The view from a particular point or from a building.

Quantity Surveyor. Primarily a measurer and compiler of materials and labours in construction works, but also an expert on cost and economic aspects of construction.

Shape. Two-dimensional areas of any part of a layout, building or any object.

Street Furniture. Minor individual elements of urban design – see Chapter 9.

Sociologist. Specialist in the study of human society and group behaviour.

Soffites. The under-surfaces of any part of a building or structure.

Sophisticated. An overworked word, not surprisingly originally meaning deprived of simplicity and misleading!, used here to mean ultra complicated and complex, although not necessarily ineffective, uses of advanced technology.

Structure. (1) Any large construction other than a building; (2) the essential physical part of any design.

Structural Engineer. A specialist in the efficient and economic design of structures – see (2) above – especially foundations, supporting walls, columns and beams, floors and roofs.

Structural System. A distinct principle of construction – see Chapter 11.

Style. Appearance of buildings or objects having marked characteristics or fashionable features of a particular period or locality.

Stylistic. In the manner of a previous style.

Symmetry. Repetition of parts of a design about an axis.

Synthesis. Putting together of elements to make a whole design to meet fully the requirements of the brief.

Technology (Advanced). The using of means and methods involving complex machines, electronic devices and mathematical processes to achieve desired practical ends.

Thermal Movement. Movement in buildings and structures caused by expansion and contraction due to varying atmospheric temperature.

Townscape. Street or urban scenes generally.

Urban Design. The general design of groups of buildings and associated structures, roads and open spaces forming parts of towns.

Wirescape. The chaotic webs of cables, aerials and their supports that disfigure the skylines of many towns.

Zone. An area, urban or rural, primarily restricted to one kind of development or use.

Index

141